T0365524

Shatter Me With Dawn

The Transcendent Experience
of Emily Dickinson

RC Allen

EDITED BY
JANICE L DEWEY

 www.trafford.com

North America & international
toll-free: 1 888 232 4444 (USA & Canada)
phone: 812 355 4082

Also by RC Allen

To Belita, Mark, Katie, & Eric

323

As if I asked a common Alms,
And in my wondering hand
A Stranger pressed a Kingdom,
And I, bewildered, stand –
As if I asked the Orient
Had it for me a Morn –
And it should lift its purple dikes,
And shatter me with Dawn!

306

The Soul's Superior instants
Occur to Her – alone –
When friend – & Earth's occasion
Have infinite withdrawn –

Or She – Herself – ascended
To too remote a Height
For lower Recognition
Than Her Omnipotent –

This Mortal Abolition
Is seldom – but as fair
As Apparition – subject
To Autocratic Air –

Eternity's disclosure
To favorites – a few –
Of the Colossal substance
Of Immortality

CONTENTS

INTRODUCTION: ED IN THE DHARMA

Nor any know I know the Art I mention – easy – Here –

(From P-326)

"The Soul's Superior instants," (P-306) is the clearest description of ego-transcendence that anyone could want. There is nothing ambiguous about it, there are no "cryptic" expressions, no possible alternative meanings. It is one more of the countless descriptions of the dharma experience that have been recorded down through the ages. This brings up the obvious question: Why have none of Dickinson's commentators ever recognized what she is talking about?

The answer must lie in the kind of readers led to devote their time to Emily Dickinson & her poetry. These have been, for the most part, academics thoroughly egocentric in their view of reality. This is not unusual, since virtually everybody is "thoroughly egocentric."

It never occurs to such people that there is an alternative to the way they see reality, their ontology. This is so, even if they are old enough to have lived through the years of the counterculture, the psychedelic hippie era. During the 60s & 70s American college students "turned on," & created a subculture based on a new ontology: non-ego awareness. This was triggered by a number of mind-changing substances, including cannabis, LSD, magic mushrooms, & peyote. This was the era of the "generation gap." The definition of "generation gap" in John McCleary's Hippie Dictionary is worth quoting in full:

Generation gap a difference in age & values. The phenomenon in which young & old are unable to communicate rationally with each other. Most often caused by a difference of opinion on moral & social issues brought about by opposing perspectives on what is important in life. The moral idealism & decadence of youth are often in conflict with the desires for security & stability harbored by mature adults.*

At the time of the generation gap I was a middle-aged college prof. As a transcendentalist by temperament, I quickly identified with the younger side of the gap, & with the transcendentalist ontology embraced by the hippie culture. For some years I had been studying Zen, & its relevance to the poetry of the Spanish transcendentalist poets. The new, psychedelic culture reflected an empirical grasp & excited enjoyment of Hindu & Buddhist ontology.

All of this happened to me during the 70s & 80s. In 1985 I took early retirement & moved to Northampton, Massachusetts. This was for personal reasons unrelated to transcendentalism; but the move proved karmic, for I suddenly found myself living next door to Amherst, & was drawn to visit the Dickinson Homestead many times. I began to read Dickinson's poetry & when I came to P-306, her reference to "The Souls Superior instants" came as a revelation: Emily Dickinson lived in the dharma! She lived with a Secret Sharer whom I call ED. She kept it all hidden away, with her private stash of dharma poems.

P-306 is a sutra, an unequivocal description of the dharma. It is as clear as a windowpane. This being the case, why does ED remain invisible to her commentators? Answer: it takes one to know one. Typically, straight people don't intuit a gay presence,

---

*   The Hippie Dictionary, a 700-page volume, is a monumental overview of the counterculture, & an invaluable reference work.

& egocentric people don't intuit a transcendentalist presence. Prof. Cynthia Wolff, in her tome, <u>Emily Dickinson,</u> freely admits that she is mystified:

> Much of Dickinson's strongest poetry is inaccessible— that is, it is difficult to determine precisely what such poetry is "about." (140)

This is extraordinary; a scholar writes a tome about a subject that baffles her understanding. The result is a corpus of guesswork, making it up as you go along.

In the past half-century Dickinson has become the basis of a cottage industry fronted by the Emily Dickinson International Society. EDIS publishes a <u>Journal,</u> printed by Johns Hopkins University Press, which gains it a certain academic cachet.

Similar quasi-academic journals have long been published by enthusiastic hobbyists. In the 1970s I recall enjoying an amusing quarterly called <u>The Baker Street Journal,</u> devoted to Sherlockiana, as they called it. The contributors invented problems to be solved (such as documenting & elucidating internal contradictions found in the canon). They wrote in the spirit of playful scholarship, & had their <u>Journal</u> published by Fordham University Press.

Another such "journal" is <u>The Baum Bugle: A Journal of Oz.</u> This is a publication by people who cherish their childhood love of the Oz Books. These people are not satirical; they are seriously nostalgic, & they treat their materials with a straitlaced scholarly attitude, as evidenced by <u>The Annotated Road to Oz,</u> which ran serially.

The <u>Journal</u> of the Emily Dickinson International Society is a similar publication, a quarterly written by hobbyists. They make no distinction between the persona of Emily Dickinson & the persona who speaks in her "enigmatic" poetry, nor do they question what makes it enigmatic. They entertain a conventional view of Dickinson as a talented woman, who wrote poetry, wrote letters, gardened, & baked bread. It does not occur to them that there is an elephant in their parlor. This is ED in the dharma.

If ED's poetry baffles her fans, it is because non-ego discourse in general is alien to ego-understanding. Ego-transcendence reveals a reality that contradicts the conventional worldview. It is what ED calls "The Truth's superb surprise" in her famous P-1129, "Tell all the Truth but tell it slant." Enlightenment immediately gives birth to a new value system, a "transvaluation of values," & one begins to speak paradoxically, as in P-1017:

> To die—without the Dying
> And live—without the Life
> This is the hardest Miracle
> Propounded to Belief.

This baffles ego-understanding, but makes perfect sense to one who has awakened by undergoing ego-death. Ego can know nothing of an awareness achieved through its own brief demise — hence the bafflement of ED's readers.

Satori, as it is called in Zen Buddhism, strikes like lightning, & shatters not only one's ingrained worldview, but one's very sense of self; the ego-identity is a passing fancy as it were. The young Dickinson was a naïve & provincial girl/woman isolated in a nineteenth-century New England village, so the repeated bolts out of the blue were bound to leave her reeling, frightened, & traumatized, as she attests in P-362:

> It struck me – every Day –
> The Lightning was as new
> As if the Cloud that instant slit
> And let the Fire through –

It burned Me – in the Night –
It blistered to My Dream –
It sickened fresh upon my sight –
With every Morn that came –

Yet, she had awakened to a new Self-identity. She found herself reborn as witness/poet, & so began a secret, thirty-five-year career as the unknown Buddha of Amherst.

By now the reader will readily see how & why the present study is organized as it is. Dickinson suffered a shocking existential challenge, & rose to the occasion. In this sense her poetry is the result of post-traumatic stress syndrome; initially she feared it might be a "disorder" – but ED quickly took the helm & kept Dickinson on course for the rest of her life.

I. PROLOGUE

THE WITNESS WHO EXPLAINS

I cannot want it more —
I cannot want it less —
My Human Nature's fullest force
Expends itself on this.

(From P-1301)

THE WITNESS WHO EXPLAINS: EMILY DICKINSON AS ED

Emily Dickinson, at a young age, experienced enlightenment. She suddenly awoke from the ego-illusion of time & place where she saw "New Englandly" (P-285), & found herself in the transcendent, non-ego reality that the Buddhists call the dharma. In the absence of any cultural ego-self, all things are experienced in their "suchness." This is the original habitat of human consciousness before the child becomes "socialized." It is Dickinson's "Eden." We commonly experience this kind of suchness in our dreams, when the diminished ego-self is no longer in charge of our awareness: it sits in the amen corner & admires the oneiric reality. In similar fashion Dickinson's Higher Self—ED—experiences a transcendent ontology which she calls by many names (Bliss, Exhilaration, Rapture, Intoxication, etc.); the Buddhists call it nirvana, "ego-extinction."

This "new" reality creates a spiritual seesaw, Dickinson/ED, called "Mutual Monarch" in P-642:

Me from Myself – to banish –
Had I Art –
Impregnable my Fortress
Unto All Heart –

But since Myself – assault Me –
How have I peace
Except by subjugating
Consciousness?

And since We're mutual Monarch
How this be
Except by Abdication –
Me – of Me?

ED recognizes the conflicted situation by using the singular, not the plural – "Mutual Monarch," not "Mutual Monarchs" – because they are two-in-one, like the Christian Father/Son. There is no "split personality," much less any "alter ego," since ED is non-ego awareness. Unlike most of us, ED is a whole person precisely because she experiences both little self & Big Self – a goal now earnestly pursed in this country by the American Buddhists devoted to the practice of formal meditation.

Formal meditation can lead to a sudden flash of enlightenment, when one awakens from the ego-illusion. This satori, as the Zen Buddhists call it, sometimes happens to unsuspecting, egocentric people innocent of any knowledge of, or interest in, the phenomenon. In our own time it happened to Eckhart Tolle, now well known in New Age circles for his books on Enlightenment (e.g., The Power of Now). In nineteenth-century New England it happened to Emily Dickinson, probably in adolescence. She rose to the occasion & became a Witness/Poet, like Rumi, or Kahlil Gibran. She devoted the rest of her life (some 35 years) to an inspired discourse regarding little self & Big Self — the ego-dominant mode (Dickinson), & the ego-transcendent mode (ED).

Living at the time of our Civil War, ED readily saw her own internal struggle as such a conflict, as she describes in P-594:

> The Battle fought between the Soul
> And No Man — is the One
> Of all the Battles prevalent —
> By far the Greater One —
>
> No News of it is had abroad —
> Its Bodiless Campaign
> Establishes, & terminates —
> Invisible — Unknown —

ED came to understand & to discourse on the ins & outs of this that was happening, the lifelong process called Individuation (after Jung). A great many of her poems — perhaps the bulk of them — concern this psychological seesaw. She came to see how small children are living in a "pre-ego" world; how they become "socialized," & learn to identify with a social ego-self contingent upon time & place; how, as one matures, this social self may be transcended, allowing the creative inner, unique Individual to emerge. Throughout her oeuvre ED touches on all these themes. In P-959, for example, she describes how, in retrospect, she was dimly aware, as a little girl, that "socialization: was cutting her off from something valuable:

> A loss of something ever felt I —
> The first that I could recollect
> Bereft I was — of what I knew not
> Too young that any should suspect

A Mourner walked among the children
I notwithstanding went about
As one bemoaning a Dominion
Itself the only Prince cast out –

She felt "bereft," but was unable to identify her loss, because that is what "socialization" is all about. Ego, by definition, is amnesiac. And of course ED was so young at the time, that nobody would have been able to detect any behavioral oddity such as marked ED's manner in later years.

P-728 is an unusually accessible poem in which Dickinson addresses ED, concerning the "socialization" that alienated them originally:

Let Us play Yesterday –
I – the Girl at school –
You – & Eternity – the
Untold Tale –

Easing my famine
At my Lexicon –
Logarithm – had I – for Drink –
'Twas a dry Wine –

Here Dickinson recounts the beginnings of her Self-creation as ED. This process is discussed by Stephen Batchelor, one of the elders of the American Buddhist movement. He cites the doctrine of Mhayana Buddhism wherein the "Buddhahood" is fully realized not at the moment of awakening, but only when the awakened imagination begins to creatively emanate images.

In fact, the practice of dharma is more truly akin to the practice of art. With the tools of ethics, meditation, & understanding, one works the clay of one's confined & anguished existence into a bodhisattva. Practice is a process of self-creation.*

Such was the creation of ED's dharma poetry: Dickinson worked "the clay of [her] confined & anguished existence" into the oracular voice of ED.

In P-680 ED assesses the Individuation Process. Like Jung, she assesses it in the only way possible – through personal experience:

> Each Life Converges to some Centre –
> Expressed – or still –
> Exists in every Human Nature
> A Goal –

Formal meditation is commonly thought of as Centering. Ego is "eccentric" (ex-centric) with regard to Psyche. The will to find one's Center is basic to the Individuation Process, living one's life with an ever-deepening connection with Psyche & the creative unconscious. Thus one discovers & lives one's Higher (or Deeper) Self. Thus did Dickinson discover & live ED.

NEW VALUES, NEW STRATEGIES

It is clear enough from her poetry that throughout her life ED experienced episodes of satori, presumably without any attempt to practice formal meditation. In any case, she lived her everyday life mindfully, never more so than when gardening; so it comes as no surprise that she should describe ego-transcendence as it is experienced in ritual meditation. In our Introduction we have commented briefly on P-306, where ED observes that

---

*   Tricycle, (Winter 1994), 71.

The Soul's Superior instants
Occur to Her – alone –
When friend – & Earth's occasion
Have infinite withdrawn –

To empty the mind means to allow thoughts of other people
("friend") & worldly activity ("Earth's occasion") to withdraw,
to be "infinite withdrawn." This is no easy task. It is daunting
to people with strong egos, but these are people who have no
interest in meditating, because it has no use, serves no function.
The transcendentalist knows better; ED's own experience taught
her this, as she observes in P-677:

To be alive – is Power –
Existence – in itself –
Without a further function –
Omnipotence – Enough –

With the revelation of an emergent ED, Dickinson realized that
she was a marked woman. It set her apart from the egocentric
community, & alienated her from the church. Satori reveals not
only the non-existence of the ego-self, but also the non-existence
of any creator god, seen to be an ego-projection, a means of
ensuring ego's survival after death. In the insightful P-662 ED
states this clearly:

Embarrassment of one another
And God
Is Revelation's limit,
Aloud
Is nothing that is chief,
But still,
Divinity dwells under seal.

To "embarrass" means "to place in doubt, perplexity, or difficulties" (Merriam-Webster). The appearance of ED embarrassed no end the life of Emily Dickinson; but, as she slyly adds, it also embarrassed God! There is no Man Upstairs presiding over human affairs. Revelation, she says, has two possible forms: "aloud," & "still." She keeps her revelations "still," hidden away; revelation "aloud" "Is nothing that is chief," she says. Nowadays we all have ready access to her poetry; to us it is "aloud," a living voice in the land. At the same time, its oracular quality reveals nothing to the egocentric reader; there appears to be "nothing that is chief," no apparent underlying theme. Hence ED's reputation as our "cryptic," our "enigmatic" poet. Quietly, however, "Divinity dwells under seal." This means both "hidden away," & "authenticated."

Ego-transcendence creates a "transvaluation of values' that makes the ego-self a secondary priority in the living of one's life. One's value system is stood on its head: ego is not "awake," it is asleep; material wealth is poverty; ego-attachments do not enrich life, they construct it. Such being the case, Dickinson, the emergent poet, had to seek a modus operandi, & so she went into the closet. To publicize her heretical secret would be a social disaster, & early on, in P-381, she took this into account:

A Secret told –
Ceases to be a Secret – then –
A Secret – kept –
That – can appall but One –

Better of it – continual be afraid –
Than it –
And Whom you told it to – beside –

And so began her lifelong practice of turning her poetry into booklets that she stashed away, one by one, & nobody the wiser. These are the "slow Riches" of P-843:

> I made slow Riches but my Gain
> Was steady as the Sun
> And every Night, it numbered more
> Than the preceding One

The phenomenon of non-ego awareness was a constant in ED's life, so intimately a part of the way she thought & felt, that she frequently calls it "It," merely, without offering any antecedent, as in our epigraph above:

> I cannot want it more –
> I cannot want it less –
> My Human Nature's fullest force
> Expends itself on this.

This "It," this Tao, or "Way," is the transvaluation of values that ED calls in P-593, "Conversion of the Mind":

> I could not have defined the change –
> Conversion of the Mind
> Like Sanctifying in the Soul –
> Is witnessed – not explained –

She says this modestly; but as witness/poet she does indeed, over the course of the ensuing years, "explain" this Conversion of the Mind. However one chooses to understand the term "explain," over & over she accounts for it & examines its dynamics. In fact, her poetic career consists in being the Witness Who Explains.

II. EGO-TRANSCENDENCE AS TRAUMA

The manner in which Dickinson experienced satori determined the kind of discourse she adopted as witness/poet. Isolated in a nineteenth-century American village, she knew nothing of enlightenment as the goal of Eastern meditators since ancient times. In her time & place ego-loss was tantamount to madness. In any Asian village ED would have been regarded as a spiritual adept; in Amherst she was the town weirdo. She herself wrote many a poem expressing her ambivalence about satori — which is to say that Dickinson could be ambivalent about ED, as plainly stated in P-642, "Me from Myself — to banish."

Given the circumstances surrounding ED's experience, we have to recognize it as a trauma, a "wound in the order of being," creating severe emotional stress. Its aftermath is what today is called "post-traumatic stress syndrome." A new identity becomes apparent, in which the person centers his or her energy on dealing with the trauma — or on avoiding it, repressing it, & being tortured by it, especially in dreams. In this latter case the person is said to suffer from "post-traumatic stress disorder." This is best known as a common problem among military men who have been traumatized in battle. In the First World War it was called "shell shock"; in the second "combat fatigue"; later, "PTSD." It is always a "disorder," because it entails unrelieved suffering that typically leads to alcoholism, drug abuse, & not infrequently suicide.

Outside the context of war, severe trauma may create a "syndrome," not a "disorder." The sudden & unexpected loss of identity may shock one into a new & growing awareness that the old identity was good riddance. After all, in the East, among Hindus & Buddhists, "wisdom" has traditionally been contrasted to ego. Disciplined study & meditation is aimed at ego-transcendence. This has not been a tradition in the West, but there are documented cases of people shocked into ego-transcendence.

One such person is Matthew Sandford, a young American paraplegic yoga instructor who teaches from a wheelchair. When he was 13 an auto crash killed his father & sister & left him paralyzed. He came to understand that his terrible trauma must be dealt with in terms of the mind/body connection. As a human being with a human mind he realized that he did not have to let his body dictate his identity. A new identity began to take shape. He was not a "cripple," he was a person dealing with a traumatizing event. In yoga he found a way to do this, & eventually he wrote a book titled Waking: A Memoir of Trauma & Transcendence. In 2006 Utne magazine published an interview with Sanford, conducted by Nina Utne. The subject: dealing with trauma. Ms. Utne had read Sanford's book, of course, & in the interview remarked on the "paradox" of dealing with trauma: the fact that "trauma makes you fearful, but it also frees you." Sanford answered as follows:

> Part of the wisdom of trauma comes from that paradox. Trauma requires me to acknowledge that my life has been harsh. Does it hurt? Yes. At the same time, I'm desperately in love with living, with the gift of life. Healing trauma calls on us to honor the life force & not be destructive with it. Does this feeling come from sadness, too? Yes, it's both. Simultaneously, I am heart-broken & desperately in love.*

It is clear that ED's entire oeuvre is concerned with honoring the life force.

Utne's interview with Sanford is called (cleverly) "Crash Course." ED herself used the very same word in the very same context. In P-1503 she called her trauma "The Crash of nothing, yet of all," meaning that the traumatic event destroyed the naïve ego-self (her "all"), which turned out to be "nothing." In P-997 she calls this "Crash's law."

---

* Utne (July-Aug '06), 49.
See poems 274, 281, 381, 512, 673.

SHATTERED BY DAWN

975

The Mountain sat upon the Plain
In his tremendous Chair –
His observation omnifold,
His inquest, everywhere –

The Seasons played around his knees
Like Children round a sire –
Grandfather of the Days is He
Of Dawn, the Ancestor –

THE INQUEST

To the transcendentalist, the Mountain is always Magic, the archetype of the human ascent along the path of self-realization. This can be a daunting climb, as ED notes in P-1507, apostrophizing Buddha Mind:

> Efface the mountain with your face
> And catch me ere I drop

The present poem is written in the past tense, as if to sum up an observation made over the course of years:

> The Mountain sat upon the Plain
> In his tremendous Chair –
> His observation omnifold,
> His inquest, everywhere –

The "tremendous Chair" in which the Mountain sits is the milieu of earth & heaven – he sits in it, not on it – & so connotes "Chair" in the sense of "official seat," as in "cathedral," from L. cathedra, "chair."

Line three, "His observation omnifold," presents ED's heavy-duty coinage, "omnifold." "Fold," in the geological sense, is the "bend of flexure produced in rock by forces operative after the deposit.. of the rock" [Merriam-Webster]. In other words, the formation of mountains is "omnifold," marked throughout by stressed bends in the earth's crust. Because of this, the mountain's "observation" is omnifold (or manifold). A mountain is regarded as an observation point offering a panoramic view enfolding earth & sky.

The key word in this poem is "inquest," marking a focused "observation" on the part of ED herself. An inquest is commonly thought of as an official investigation of the cause of a death — a coroner's inquest. This connotation is certainly connected with the meaning of the second stanza:

> The Seasons played around his knees
> Like Children round a sire –
> Grandfather of the days is He
> Of Dawn, the Ancestor –

"Dawn" is, of course, the archetype of Enlightenment; & when ED calls the mountain the "Ancestor" of Dawn, this is her word for "archetype."

Ego-transcendence entails ego-death, by definition. When one awakens in the reality of unconditioned awareness, or nirvana ("ego-extinction"), one is standing at the top of the mountain as it were, able to contemplate the cause of this shattering of ego. This is ED's inquest into how Dickinson was shattered with Dawn.

981

As Sleigh Bells seem in summer
Or Bees, at Christmas show –
So fairy – so fictitious
The individuals do
Repealed from observation –
A Party that we knew –
More distant in an instant
Than Dawn in Timbuctoo.

DISTANT IN AN INSTANT

This poem appears to be a simple observation that we have all made; namely, that people —even close friends—can suddenly reveal a hidden side hitherto unsuspected. The classic case is the sudden murder: a mournful peaceful & law-abiding citizen unexpectedly, without warning, commits murder, & the neighbors all say, "That's not like him." He or she is "Repealed from observation," as ED puts it: the "personality" we thought we knew is revoked forever,

> More distant in an instant
> Than Dawn in Timbuctoo.

Early on I learned to take special note of ED's epigrammatic poems that seem to be mere truisms. She was living an inner revolution, & creating an original discourse grounded in her own empirical experience of Psyche. Taking this into consideration, I came to understand that a poem like the present one is about ED's own unique life experience, her inner revolution. ED does not write about "what we all know"; she writes about what she herself has inwardly discovered. So far as she is concerned, nobody else knows this.

Seen in this light, the present poem is autobiographical. ED is making a contrast between the known ego-self, & the unknown transcendent Self. She is articulating her own amazement at the difference between Emily Dickinson & ED. When satori entered the life of Emily Dickinson, ED was born. In an "instant" she was as distant from Emily Dickinson as Dawn in Timbuktu. "Dawn" means Enlightenment which, for ego, is Timbuktu. Nobody knows where Timbuktu actually is — which is the point. When Lightning struck, Dickinson was "Repealed from observation." When ED awoke, Dickinson was "A Party that we knew" — the Party of the first part, now strangely distant from spiritual truth. ED is the Party of the second Part.

87

A darting fear – a pomp – a tear –
A waking on a morn
To find that what one waked for,
Inhales the different dawn.

THE DIFFERENT DAWN

The definite article in line 4 is key: "Inhales the different dawn." It indicates that here are two dawns — the usual dawn, & the different dawn, sunrise & Enlightenment. It was this different dawn that shattered. It created ED's ambivalence, given her provincialism, unaware of satori as a coveted goal of Eastern meditators. In her time & place ego-loss generated a fear of madness, as in P-410, "Could it be Madness — this?" In the present poem ED states that she experienced "A darting fear — a pomp — a tear." There is the pomp of her coronation (see P-356, "The Day that I was crowned", & the fear of ego-loss which, elsewhere, she calls "appalling" (P-281). Likewise, in P-673 she says:

> 'Tis this — invites — appalls — endows —
> Flits — glimmers — proves — dissolves —
> Returns — suggests — convicts — enchants —
> Then — flings in Paradise —

The present poem, in four terse lines, has as its subject the ambivalence of it all.

Satori reveals the Breath of Life as the omnipotent Spirit of Vitality. This is why, in the present poem, ED says that she "Inhales the different dawn;" likewise, in P-1382, she describes satori as "a sumptuous Destitution" (i.e., devoid of ego) that one has "inhaled":

Profane it by a search – we cannot
It has no home –
Nor we who having once inhaled it –
Thereafter roam.

This is "what one waked for," meaning awakening to Buddha Mind.

1079

The Sun went down – no Man looked on –
The Earth & I, alone,
Were present at the Majesty –
He triumphed, & went on –

The Sun went up – no Man looked on –
The Earth & I & One
A nameless Bird – a Stranger
Were Witness for the Crown –

THE SUN WENT UP

This poem has long impressed me as the locus classicus of ED's self-identification (or Self-identification) as Witness/Poet. In the first stanza, concerning sunset, she is "alone" with Earth:

> The Sun went down – no Man looked on –
> The Earth & I, alone,
> Were present at the Majesty –
> He triumphed, & went on –

This is the transcendent loneliness or solitude, where one has tuned out the chattering ego-self, just as occurs in a successful meditation.* When ED says "no Man looked on," this includes her own conscious ego-self.** This was a magical sunset, not because it was spectacular, but because her transcendent awareness experience enlightenment as the Majesty of Light. Satori is a great "triumph" of human consciousness (just as compassion is the concomitant triumph of human feeling).

The second stanza concerns dawn:

---

* See <u>Solitary Prowess</u>, "True Loneliness," 188-189.

** "Man" was commonly generic in the language of that time, & ED does not hesitate to refer to herself in the "masculine," as in poems 389, 801, 986, 1466, & 1487.

The Sun went up – no Man looked on –
The Earth & I & One
A nameless Bird – a Stranger
Were Witness for the Crown –

Again she experiences the transcendent solitude, of the same quality, as indicated by her iteration (lines 1-2, 5-6). ED's use of "nameless" here is crucial to her meaning. In the absence of ego, names & labels lose their importance. Thoreau, as a natural-born naturalist, was very much aware of names of flora & fauna as a limited means of relating to Nature. He speaks of this at length in his Journal, & says, among other things,

> To know the names of creatures is only a convenience to us at first, but so soon as we have learned to distinguish them, the sooner we forget their names the better, so far as any true appreciation of them is concerned. ... The name is convenient in communicating with other, but it is not to be remembered when I communicate with mystery. (2-18-1860)

So ED's use of "nameless" is not vague padding, as when we say "a nameless dread," or "a nameless hunger." The bird in this poem was likely not "nameless" at all in her ego-dominant mode; but now it presents itself as an original presence, "a Stranger."

The last line is really a punch line: "Were Witness for the Crown." ED's puns are always pleasing. Here she uses a phrase from English jurisprudence; her own "Crown" is, of course, ego-transcendence, as in P-356, "The day that I was crowned."

Enlightenment is the New Dawn that shatters forever the rigid structure of the ego-dominant identity, ushering in a New Dispensation. In the present poem, from her middle years, ED shows a comfortable acceptance of that original, frightening event.

SATORI THE SHATTERER

To the serious meditator, satori may represent a goal, rightly or wrongly. It may come as a sudden liberation, inspired by disciplined desire, or perhaps by living day & night with a koan. In any case, to people on the Path enlightenment does not come as a psychic trauma.

On the other hand, satori can & does happen to innocent bystanders who may have little or no intimate knowledge of Eastern philosophies. Thus it happened to Emily Dickinson, a naive & provincial young woman—likely adolescent—who knew not what to make of it. She embraced it privately, & devoted the rest of her life to her secret task as witness/poet, seeking to discover what, indeed, she could make of it, after all.

Satori takes as many different forms as there are people. To judge by ED's descriptions, her episodes (the early ones, at least) were frightening, as she felt herself in the grip of a fearsome & inexplicable psychic upheaval. These episodes left her spent with anxiety concerning the state of her mental balance. To make matters worse, the experience isolated her, for there was no one with whom she could confidently share the heretical secret, as she confesses in P-381, "A Secret told - / Ceases to be a Secret" (see above, "The Witness Who Explains," p. 3).

The following selection of poems presents ED's "satorical" discourse wherein she narrates & evaluates her changing impressions of what it all seemed to signify, as more & more it became a permanent part of who she was. Like it or not, she found herself profoundly engaged in one of the most incredible & least understood vocations in the history of American letters.

P-1517, "How much of Source escapes with thee."

This poem, a late one, states the original sense of loss, when first ED awoke in an egoless world. The universe grown familiar to her from childhood had vanished along with the ego-self of her accustomed life.

P-42, "A Day! Help! Help! Another Day!"
This poem, one of her earliest, features a series of exclamations, as of a woman in distress. The punctuation is a rarity for her. She pictures the traumatic loss as a dire crisis in her young life, one that requires a distress signal, a red alert to her community; at the same time she is able to see that she may have panicked needlessly. (Perhaps she later decided that she had also punctuated needlessly).

P-426, "It don't sound so terrible – quite – as it did."
As witness/poet ED deals with the "language of trauma," the question of how to create a discourse uniting eros & logos, instinct & intellect. She does not identify with the trauma – for that is not who she is—but rather "accustoms" herself to examine it & its aftermath.

P-281, "'Tis so appalling – it exhilarates."
She understands & accepts her divided consciousness as the starting point for the discourse to come. There is "Torment"; but again, "Torment: is not who she is. There is pain, but she does not "hallow" it (as she puts it in P-772), i.e., does not incorporate it into her identity, as a martyr might do. Much like the practitioners of Insight Meditation (vipassana), she observes & reports.

P-280, "I felt a Funeral in my Brain," & P-712, "Because I could not stop for Death."
Both these poems, among her best known, are detailed, metaphorical descriptions of ego-death, presented as rituals marking the irreversibility of the trauma.

P-314, "Nature – sometimes sears a Sapling," P-362, "It struck me – every Day, " P-925m "Struck, was I, not yet by Lightning," & P-315m "He fumbles at your Soul."

These four poems attest to the violence of ED's awakening —perhaps a series of episodes—as a destructive electrical storm.

P-739, "I many times thought Peace had come," & P-1113, "There is a strength in proving that it can be borne."

These two poems portray Psyche as a storm-tossed ship challenging the best efforts of her crew.

P-997, "Crumbling is not an instant's Act," & P-1123, "A great Hope fell."

Here ED surveys the decaying ruins of what once appeared to be a solid edifice. Most people never have reason to doubt the solidity of this egocentric construction.

P-1490, "The Face in evanescence lain."

ED comes to grasp the reality of impermanence (anicca) as revealing the non-existence of the ego-self: Enlightenment is recognized as "Detriment Divine."

P-180, "As if some little Arctic flower."

This, the last poem of the section, evokes the peace after the storm, like the slow movement of Beethoven's Pastoral Symphony.

1517

How much of Source escapes with thee –
How chief thy sessions be –
For thou hast borne a universe
Entirely away.

All things swept sole away
This – is immensity –
(1512)

THE CRASH OF NOTHING

"Ego-transcendence" means transcendence of the ego-reality, the everyday ontology that we all take for granted: ego "in here," & the world "out there." Reginald Ray, professor of Buddhist studies at Naropa University, describes it like this:

> Ultimately, the apparent duality of subject & object is not given in reality. It is a structure that we... impose on the world. When we see the phenomenal world truly as it is, we realize a level of being that precedes the subject-object split.*

In P-1503 ED describes satori as concisely as possible: The Crash of nothing, yet of all." That is to say, the relative world of ego is seen to be an illusion, a "nothing," & it is this that "crashes" when we transcend it. It breaks & goes to pieces, just as described in P-474:

> It dropped so low – in my Regard–
> I heard it hit the Ground –
> And go to pieces on the Stones
> At the bottom of my Mind –

---

* Shambhala sun (Jan., 2001), 71.

In the present poem ED sums it up again;

> How much of Source escapes with thee –
> How chief thy sessions be –
> For thou hast borne a universe
> Entirely away.

Apostrophizing Buddha Mind (ED), she refers to episodes of satori as "sessions." "Source" is a key word in this poem. I take it in its relative meaning, "point of origin," as in P-285 ("The Robin's my Criterion for Tune"), where Dickinson says of "The Queen" (ED)"

> Because I see – New Englandly –
> The Queen, discerns like me –
> Provincially –

(Cf. the "Phantom Queen" of P-346.) Because New England is Dickinson's point of origin, its culture is the source of her idiomatic, provincial discourse. This is the Source that "escapes," that is transcended; the ego-reality of her time & place is merely "a universe," one of many; Enlightenment causes it to vanish in a trace.

42

A Day! Help! Help! Another Day! *
Your prayers, oh Passer by!
From such a common ball as this
Might date a Victory!
From marshallings as simple
The flags of nations swang.
Steady – my soul: What issues
Upon thine arrow hang!

Earlier we have quoted the "mutual Monarch" poem (682, "Me from Myself – to Banish"), & the "civil war" poem (594, "The Battle fought between the Soul / And No Man") as being clear examples of ED's life as a struggle between ego & non-ego. In the present poem, a very early one, ED voices her apprehension in the first stages of the traumatic event. Emily Dickinson, unaware of Eastern traditions regarding ego-transcendence, could not readily accept (much less name) the Event, the Crash that shattered her sense of identity. Here she sees her first reaction not in inner terms (civil war), but in outer terms. Facing a crisis, she imagines calling for outside help, sending a signal of distress, an SOS to the community.

This theme is of special interest, since among Buddhists "community" refers to the sangha, the network of fellow Buddhists. ED needed a sangha; Dickinson needed her neighbors. Her sense of the conventional, egocentric reality (I/it dual mind) had been shattered, & needed to be reconfirmed & reinforced by the common wisdom. The "appalling" event created an ego-fear crying out, "Mayday!" Anyone at all –the first "Passer by"–could bring her back into samsara, the comfortable world of ego-reality.

But ED quickly asserts her Presence as the one to answer an SOS, & she says reassuringly, "Steady – my soul!" (line 7).

Using the metaphor of war, ED describes her satori as a bullet wound:

> From such a common ball as this
> Might date a Victory!

Lines 1-2 give voice to Dickinson's immediate panic reaction; lines 3-4 mean, "Don't panic!" "Steady, my soul!"

In ED's time, the time of our Civil war, "ball" was the projectile fired by a muzzle-loading weapon. This is how ED uses the term in P-159:

A *Sailor's* business is *the shore*!
A *Soldier's* – *balls!*

In the present poem ED calls the Event "a common ball."
By this I understand "a wound (trauma) that could happen to
anybody" – just as in battle the common soldier is vulnerable
("liable to suffer a wound [L. vulnus]")

Dickinson's ambivalence concerning the traumatic event allows
her to intuit "victory," as in P-103:

> And Bells keep saying "Victory"
> From steeples in my soul!

A soldier who falls in battle might believe that his sacrifice is part
of the larger victory. ED is able to see that the trauma was simply
a "marshalling," an inspired new way of deploying the elements
of Psyche. On such genius in the battlefield may victory depend,
leading to an open recognition of the new dispensation:

> From marshallings as simple
> The flags of nations swang.

(I take "swang" to be "swung," i.e., unfurled, flying in the breeze.)
In the final two lines ED speaks calmly to Dickinson:

> Steady – my soul: What issues
> Upon thine arrow hang!

"Don't panic, don't jump to conclusion." The "rifle ball" is
exchanged for "arrow," perhaps with the thought of Eros – for
satori is, finally, the victory of Eros over Logos, ego-intellect. It
is the arrow in the heart that does not kill, but awakens.

All the "issues" that hang upon this arrow are issues that will
be addressed throughout ED's poetic career.

426

It don't sound so terrible – quite – as it did –
I run it over – "Dead", Brain, "Dead."
Put it in Latin – left of my school –
Seems it don't shriek so – under rule.

Turn it, a little – full in the face
A Trouble looks bitterest –
Shift it – just –
Say "When tomorrow comes this way –
I shall have waded down one day."

I suppose it will interrupt me some
Till I get accustomed – but then the Tomb
Like other new Things – shows largest – then –
And smaller, by Habit –

It's shrewder then
Put the Thought in advance – a Year –
How like "a fit" – then –
Murder – wear!

"MURDER," SHE WROTE

Alfred Habegger, in his biography of Dickinson, identifies this poem as one of the "few poems that explicitly touch on the [Civil War], such as... were inspired by fatalities."* This may or may not be the case; the poem is not included in the recent collection of ED's supposed Civil War poems (nineteen in all) appearing in Words For the Hour: A New Anthology of American Civil War Poetry.**

The fact does not surprise me, since the present poem is written in a breezy, offhand style, concerning the function of words as these relate to actual experience. What has this got to do with the Civil War, or indeed, with any war? ED says here that you can get used to death by regarding it as a threatening idea, as an abstract word:

> It don't sound so terrible – quite – as it did –
> I run it over – "Dead", Brain, "Dead."
> Put it in Latin – left of my school –
> Seems it don't shriek so – under rule.

To describe an experience in so many words is to put it "under rule" – the rule of language, logos. Death may come to be "just an idea," a harmless surrogate for the real thing.

This poem may have been inspired by some event or other

---

* My Wars Are Laid Away in Books, 403.

** This anthology is co-edited by Cristanne Miller, editor of the Journal published by the Emily Dickinson International Society.

in Dickinson's daily life; in any case, the real issue is how she processed it mentally, according to her own unique inner experience of matters existential, the stresses & strains within her own psyche. The actual subject of this poem concerns the way one accustoms oneself to any sudden inner trauma, "bitter trouble" within the economy of one's own psyche:

> Turn it, a little – full in the face
> A Trouble looks bitterest –
> Shift it – just –
> Say "When Tomorrow comes this way –
> I shall have waded down one Day."

Something that once seemed "so terrible" (line 1) gradually loses its power to terrorize:

> I suppose it will interrupt me some
> Till I get accustomed – but then the Tomb
> Like other new Things – shows largest – then –
> And smaller, by Habit –

This is all spoken in a matter-of-fact way; & with a calm lack of concern she finally reveals that she is talking about "Murder":

> It's shrewder then
> Put the Thought in advance – a Year –
> How like "a fit" – then –
> Murder – wear!

Her concern here with language ("Put it in Latin") is inherent to her vocation as witness/poet. Her psyche was shattered by satori, & she awakened to the need to illuminate this traumatic event through the medium of words; writing for readers to come, one puts the thought "in advance – a Year."

P-925 is a prime example of her "language of trauma:"

> Struck, was I, not yet by Lightning –
>
> Maimed – was I – yet not by Venture –
>
> Robbed – was I – intact to Bandit –
> All my Mansion torn –
>
> Most – I live the cause that slew Me.
> Often as I die

In the last two lines of the present poem, ED reveals not only that she is speaking of murder, but, more importantly, that it is her job to fit the word to the deed:

> How like "a fit" – then –
> Murder – wear!

As witness/poet she fully understands that any poem she writes must fit word to the deed – the "deed" being satori. In P-1109 she grandly puns on this word "fit":

> I fit for them –
> I seek the Dark
> Till I am thorough fit.

(I take "them" to mean her readers – you & me. She was indeed thoroughly fit for the job.)

In general, then, the present poem concerns Dickinson's "getting accustomed" to ED: "I suppose it will interrupt me some / Till I get accustomed" (line 10-11). She has already broached this theme in P-351, her "mirror poem":

> I felt my life with both my hands
> To see if it was there –
> I held my spirit to the Glass,
> To prove it possibler –

In the final stanza she writes,

> I told myself, "Take Courage, Friend –
> That – was a former time –
> But we might learn to like the Heaven,
> As well as our Old Home!"

Initially, satori appeared to be a violent attack on ego – murder, if you like, when, on her path in life, she was waylaid by a highway robber, the "waylaying Light" of P-1581. That shocking experience takes some getting used to, especially for a Westerner innocent of the ins & outs of satori as discussed & analyzed by countless Eastern adepts.

281

'Tis so appalling – it exhilarates –
So over Horror, it half Captivates –
The Soul stares after it, secure –
A Sepulchre, fears frost, no more –

To scan a Ghost, is faint –
But grappling, conquers it –
How easy, Torment, now –
Suspense kept sawing so –

The Truth, is Bald, & Cold –
But that will hold –
If any are not sure –
We show them – prayer –
But we, who know,
Stop hoping, now –

Looking at Death, is Dying –
Just let go the Breath –
And not the pillow at your Cheek
So Slumbereth –

Others, Can wrestle –
Yours, is done –
And so of Woe, bleak dreaded – come,
It sets the Fright at liberty –
And Terror's free –
Gay, Ghastly, Holiday!

"Speech" – is a prank of *Parliament* –
"Tears" – a trick of the *nerve*
But the Heart with the heaviest freight on –
Doesn't - always – move –
(P-688)

THE AMBIVALENCE OF NAÏVE SATORI

ED was not only an accidental Buddhist; sometimes she was a very reluctant Buddhist. Her awakening came freighted with problems both inner & outer. Outwardly there was a major social problem: how to live a double life? She acknowledges this in a late poem, P-1737:

> Burden – borne so far triumphant –
> None suspect me of the crown,

For some thirty-five years she wrote her dharma poetry, stashed it away, & nobody was the wiser. This was her "letter to the World" (P-441), to be delivered posthumously.

Subjectively ED also lived a double life, a divided consciousness. This was a heroic feat, considering that she was isolated in a nineteenth-century New England village steeped in Christianity & devoted to a Creator God. In those circumstances, sudden ego-loss readily appears as madness, as a nightmare, or as an acute anxiety dream. The "exhilaration" of satori is offset by its "appalling" threat. ED's heroism lies in her determination to stay the course, even though she had no outside support. She was forced to find the Inner Guru. She lived in an egocentric community, & to confess her "heresy" ("there is no Creator God") was unthinkable.

So the opening line of the present poem states the distress

of her ambivalence: "'Tis so appalling – it exhilarates." I call this experience "naïve satori." By "naïve" I mean "without informed judgment." With time this will change considerably.

"So over Horror, it half Captivates." This "half" expresses her ambivalence. One thinks of the acrophobic standing on the edge of a cliff: he is literally "so over horror," & is "half" captivated by it – hypnotized as it were. The horror of ego-extinction is captivating – yet <u>nirvana</u> is what the Buddha called ego-extinction. It is liberation from the woe of living as an ego-self. Woe, or suffering, is the lot of ego, just as Bliss, or nirvana, is the lot of ego-transcendence, as stated in P-1168:

> As old as Woe –
> How old is that?
> Some eighteen thousand years –
> As old as Bliss
> How old is that
> They are of equal years

When satori happens to the naïve person, as to an innocent bystander, so to speak, then there is a confused reaction, as ED says in lines 3-8 of the present poem:

> The Soul stares after it, secure –
> A Sepulchre, fears frost, no more –
>
> To scan a Ghost, is faint –
> But grappling, conquers it –
> How easy, Torment, now –
> Suspense kept sawing so –

The Soul feels "secure," but the ego-self is tormented by confusion. With physical death, the coldness of the grave is all there is to fear, nothing else ("no more"); with the experience of ego-death, the Soul may be captivated by the episode, but the ego-self is appalled. This is akin to the ambivalence felt by naïve people who take LSD for the first time, perhaps as a lark: it precipitates a powerful loss of ego that threatens to be irreversible, & they freak out. They think that they have lost their mind, not gained it. This is why they need a sitter – but ED had no sitter to consult. Facing a divided consciousness she now senses the presence of a "Ghost." You can deal with a ghost by facing it squarely; but satori casts into doubt the whole question of who "you" are. Who is the ghost – ego, or non-ego? Who is grappling with whom?

"Torment" is now the prevailing mode, because "Suspense kept sawing so." I take "sawing" in the carpenter's sense: satori sawing away at her integrity of mind, threatening to sever it.

> The Truth, is Bald, & Cold –
> But that will hold –
> If any are not sure –
> We show them – prayer –

The Truth of satori "is Bald, & Cold." Liberation from ego, the realization of Emptiness, is the bald, cold truth, & it will "hold." Those who only suspect or intuit the bald truth –the atheists, the agnostics, the freethinkers—such as these, "We show them – prayer," ("We" meaning the Mainstream).

> But we, who know,
> Stop hoping, now –

If you have experienced ego-death for real, a powerful satori, you stop hoping that the ego-self is real, or that it will survive death as a "soul."

This poem is an early one, written when ED was about thirty.

As a "naïve" transcendentalist she is hard put to get used to the notion of ego-death & its aftermath: call it a transcendentalist hangover. In the final two stanzas she rephrases her idea that physical death is a simple thing, by contrast to the spiritual confusion of satori:

> Looking at Death, is Dying –
> Just let go the Breath –
> And not the pillow at your Cheek
> So Slumbereth –

When "you" (ego) are dying for real, you simply go to sleep, you "breathe your last," as they say: "Just let go the Breath." Now you are at peace. Others continue the existential struggle, but for you it is done:

> Others, Can wrestle –
> Yours, is done –

People fear death; it is the "Woe" we all face. When death actually occurs, your fright is set free:

> And so of Woe, bleak dreaded – come,
> It sets the Fright at liberty –
> And Terror's free –

This is all true; but ED's last line sums up the irony of the whole idea that death "liberates" us from our terror: "Gay, Ghastly, Holiday!" Nobody is reassured by the thought that death will set their "Fright at liberty," because death means ego-extinction – & most of us would much rather live with our Fright, than be "liberated" from it.

ED's reference to liberation – "It sets the fright at liberty"—is a good example of what I call her accidental, naïve Buddhism.

She has experienced nirvana without being aware that this is the term for her experience: "ego-extinction." At the same time she immediately begins to speak of death as liberation: "It sets the Fright at liberty." She intuits that Liberation is the issue. She ends this poem by speaking ironically of death as a "Gay, Ghastly, Holiday!" "Gay" & "Ghastly" echo the first line: "exhilarates," & "appalling." In P-383 ("Exhilaration – is within") ED recognizes satori itself as a "Holiday" – not "Ghastly," but an inner intoxication. What we all call a "holiday" cannot accomplish what happens when the inner liberation from ego occurs, as stated in the final lines of P-383:

> 'Tis not of Holiday
> To stimulate a Man
> Who hath the Ample Rhine
> Within his Closet –

Satori, on the other hand, liberates you from dependence on ego-based emotions ("attachment"). It creates confusion – but at least you are alive to wrestle with this & to make poetry. This is your true Holiday, & there is nothing "Ghastly" about it.

280

I felt a Funeral, in my Brain,
And Mourners to & fro
Kept treading – treading – till it seemed
That Sense was breaking through –

And when they all were seated,
A Service, like a Drum –
Kept beating – beating – till I thought
My Mind was going numb –

And then I heard them lift a Box
And creak across my Soul
With those same Boots of Lead, again,
Then Space – began to toll,

As all the Heavens were a Bell,
And Being, but an Ear,
And I, & Silence, some strange Race
Wrecked, solitary, here –

And then a Plank in Reason, broke,
And I dropped down, & down –
And hit a World, at every plunge,
And Finished knowing – then –

WRECKED, SOLITARY, HERE

This poem concerning a psychic split will be echoed later in P-747 & P-937. This concerns ego-loss. We have noted ED's description in P-747:

> It dropped so low – in my Regard –
> I heard it hit the Ground –
> And go to pieces on the Stones
> At bottom of my Mind –

The first stanza of P-937 says:

> I felt a Cleaving in my Mind –
> As if my Brain had split –
> I tried to match it – Seam by Seam –
> But could not make them fit.

ED is describing the experience of sudden ego-loss, when ego-transcendence occurs. To a person living isolated in a provincial American village, & unaware of the phenomenology of satori, this can be a frightening experience – what ED calls, in P-381 ("A Secret told"), a Secret that "appals" her. "Ego-extinction" (nirvana) can be blissful, & it can be devastating: it can be experienced as ego-transcendence, or as ego-death. It can appear as a Beginning, or as an End; as Supreme Wisdom, or as a sorry madness – all the more so, if the person has no one to consult, a guru experienced in the ways of ego-transcendence.

Biographers may refer to Emily Dickinson's "mentor," but these were strangers to the Territory that ED would be discovering by degrees for the rest of her life. This early poem describes satori, both as Bliss, but as ego-death:

> I felt a Funeral, in my Brain,
> And Mourners to & fro
> Kept treading – treading – till it seemed
> That Sense was breaking through –

ED may well be describing a troubling dream she had, either following satori, or preceding it as a prophetic anxiety dream. A dream, after all, is not something you "think," it is an experience you "feel in your brain."

The "Mourners" are lamenting a great loss, a common symptom (like paralysis) of the anxiety dream. As in a dream, ED observes the ritual "treading" of the mourners, until the meaning, the "Sense," nearly breaks into oneiric consciousness.

In the second stanza the ritual moves on. All the mourners are seated at a great table, whereupon a drum begins to beat a dirge, such as you hear at a military funeral. Here, the "feeling" seems to give way to "numbness." With ego-transcendence one becomes "numb" to all the usual ego-sensations. These are suddenly devoid of significance; they have lost their hold on the Higher Self.

In the next scene of this dreamlike drama, "they" lift a "Box" – a coffin (as when we say a "pine box"), & in a funeral procession, convey it across her Soul: the ego-self is about to be buried alive!*

"Then Space – began to toll," says ED. This is a significant remark, deepened by stanza four;

---

* This reflects a fear –urban myth—common in the nineteenth century.

As all the Heavens were a Bell,
And Being, but an Ear,
And I, & Silence, some strange Race
Wrecked, solitary, here –

In Buddhism, ego-transcendence is traditionally described as a Bell ringing in the Empty Sky. For centuries this (along with the Polished Mirror) has been an archetype of Buddha Mind; it now appears to ED. Such is the persistence of the archetypes.

ED recognizes that she is strangely alone in the Cosmos, not in a state of Bliss, but "Wrecked, solitary, here." The ego-identity of Emily Dickinson has been "wrecked" for good, & henceforth she will live a solitary existence in Amherst.

Now the dream comes to an end:

And then a Plank in Reason, broke,
And I dropped down, & down –
And hit a World, at every plunge,
And Finished knowing – then –

This is the equivalent of saying (as we all say, when recounting a dream), "& then I woke up." In the dream, she had been situated high, "up there" – & then she woke up. This was an experience of falling back down into the world (the Woman Who Fell to Earth), & when she awoke, she "Finished knowing." Dreaming is a form of ego-transcendent knowing, & when you awaken, you "Finish knowing."

712

Because I could not stop for death –
He kindly stopped for me –
The carriage held but just Ourselves –
And Immortality.

We slowly drove – He knew no haste
And I had put away
My labor & my leisure too,
For His Civility –

We passed the School, where Children strove
At Recess – in the Ring –
We passed the Fields of Gazing Grain –
We passed the Setting Sun –

Or rather – He passed Us –
The Dews drew quivering & chill –
For only Gossamer, my Gown –
My Tippet – only Tulle –

We paused before a House that seemed
A Swelling of the Ground –
The Roof was scarcely visible –
The Cornice – in the Ground –

Since then – 'tis Centuries – & yet
Feels shorter than the Day
I first surmised the Horses' Heads
Were toward Eternity –

SATORI: A RECESS FROM EGO

As in P-465 ("I heard a Fly buzz – when I died"), ED here narrates her own death. In the former poem this appears as a deathbed scene; in the present poem, it appears as a trip in Death's Carriage.

This poem resembles P-465 in a second way, for it uses actual death as a metaphor for the ego-death of satori. This is why ED can convincingly speak of her own death, as if she had lived to tell about it. The ego-death of satori is a powerful, life-changing event, & commonly leads to a name change recognizing the new identity (e.g., Richard Alpert becomes Ram Dass).

ED begins this narration by regarding Death benignly:

> Because I could not stop for Death –
> He kindly stopped for me –
> The Carriage held but just Ourselves –
> And Immortality.

This is not the Grim Reaper imagined by ego. A great, unexpected Good occurred: she & death were alone together with "Immortality."

"Immortality," for the transcendentalist, is satori. ED describes this in detail in P-679 (Conscious am I in my Chamber"), where Consciousness is her "shapeless friend." Her honored Guest is intuited to be "Immortality," the Eternal Now: "Instinct esteem Him / Immortality."

The first line of the present poem —"Because I could not stop for Death"—deserves further commentary. If we keep in mind that "Death" means "ego-death," then we can easily understand the attitude of the American Buddhists who practice daily meditation. They, as busy people, are deliberately "stopping for death," deliberately making an effort to be alone daily with the Higher Self. ED, who presumably did not practice formal meditation, led a busy family life — but one day the experience of ego-transcendence, ego-death, "kindly stopped" for her, & took her for a ride, a "trip."

The Eternal Now is beyond clock time, as ED says in P-287, where the puppet ego ceases to function:

> A Clock stopped —
> Not the Mantel's —
> Geneva's farthest skill
> Can't put the puppet bowing —
> That just now dangled still —

There is neither "haste" nor "leisure," as ED says in the second stanza of the present poem. She "put away" her "labor" in recognition of his "Civility." When satori occurs, one is immensely grateful, as if a great favor had been bestowed.

Stanza three goes on to describe the busy world of clock time. She observes schoolchildren at recess, playing "in the Ring," which is analogous to her own "Recess" in centered consciousness. Ripening grain has come alive in her own mind as she gazes at the heavens. She "passed the Setting Sun," she says, "Or rather — He passed Us."

That is a remarkable throwaway line, "Or rather — He passed Us." Satori reveals the real difference between Ptolemy & Copernicus. Line 12, "We passed the setting Sun" implies Copernicus; line 13, "Or rather — He passed Us," implies Ptolemy.

That is to say, ego-transcendence reveals the archetypal truth of Ptolemaic astronomy, the geocentric understanding of non-ego awareness: everything in the cosmos "revolves around" (concerns, appertains to) Buddha Mind, which is human awareness as cosmic consciousness.

She begins to feel the cold, for she wasn't dressed for this trip, so suddenly did it catch her unawares. Indeed, it is a commonplace among transcendentalists that by being unaware, you become Aware: "emptying the mind" is the high purpose of formal meditation.

In stanza five ED goes on to relate that they "paused" before a tumulus that appears to be an underground tomb, or mausoleum, whose cornice seems flush with the ground.

The operative word in this passage is "paused," I believe. Satori is a brief, "posthumous" visit with Life after Death, i.e., after the ego-self is well sedated, completely "under."

In the final stanza ED says, "Since then — 'tis Centuries," meaning that it seems like centuries, given the relativity of passing time. In P-1295 she observes,

> Eternity will be
> Velocity or Pause
> At Fundamental Signals
> From Fundamental Laws.

There is a remarkable dynamic between episodes of satori & the intervening periods of clock time, as experienced by the ego-self. The Eternal Now, a "Fundamental Signal" from "Fundamental Laws," may seem to have happened centuries —nay, eons—ago, when we look back on our last trip, so far distant is the ego from satori. But then again, it can seem like only yesterday. ED says "shorter than" the day of this particular trip, when she "first surmised the Horses' Heads / Were toward Eternity." That is to say, when she became able to see that clock time <u>can be</u> headed for satori: you need clock time in order to transcend clock time. In P-1473 ED uses this same equine metaphor:

> We were listening to the seconds' Races
> And the Hoofs of the Clock –

P-712 is one of ED's best-known poems, & with good reason, for it tells a powerful symbolic story, like a fairy tale, & so may be enjoyed intuitively, even if one does not grasp its archetypal import. It is a haunting narrative, & hard to forget, like a numinous dream.

314

Nature – sometimes sears a Sapling –
Sometimes – scalps a Tree –
Her Green People recollect it
When they do not die –

Fainter Leaves – to Further Seasons –
Dumbly testify –
We – who have the Souls –
Die oftener – Not so vitally –

THE GREEN PEOPLE

This poem prefigures the later poem, P-990:

> Not all die early, dying young –
> Maturity of Fate
> Is consummated equally
> In Ages, or a Night –
>
> A Hoary Boy, I've known to drop
> Whole statured – by the side
> Of Junior of Fourscore – 'twas Act
> Not Period – that died.

P-990 is discussed in AB (pp. 22-23). There we note the dialectic between the two kinds of death: death of Act, & death of Period. Those who live out their lives in the rut of an ego-identity are living the pseudo-reality of clock time, & after a certain period of time they die. This is death of Period. Those who live in the dharma, the Now, are evolving spiritually, continually enlarging their sense of identity through interaction with the creative unconscious (Jung's "Individuation Process"). When they die, they die caught in the act of living – "living" in the sense of vital Becoming. They are not static beings.

One can see that the present poem is an early intuition of this dialectic, generated by the quantum leap from ego to non-ego. Satori is, to a certain extent, similar to being struck by lightning, as in P-315, where "He"

Deals – One – imperial – Thunderbolt –
That scalps your naked Soul –

In the aftermath of satori it is easy to see how a tree "scalped" by lightning evokes the "scalping" of the "naked Soul." This "scalping" (opening up the top of your head) is an act of Nature, just as a living tree is an act of Nature. When Nature, in the form of lightning, strikes Nature in the form of tree, this generates a "recollection" in those who survive, which is to say that ego-death leaves a permanent scar. Emily Dickinson is permanently marked as ED. The "foliage" of the ego-self –its protective canopy of habits & idiosyncrasies—becomes "Fainter," & may "Dumbly testify" to the transcendent event.

Most people die the death of Period, not the death of Act, where they would be caught in the embodiment of their vitality. Egos "Die oftener – Not so vitally." Such is my reading of the last two lines;

We – who have the Souls –
Die oftener – Not so vitally –

The generic "we," meaning "everybody," i.e., egocentric people (they are practically everybody): these are the ones with "the souls," the ones who allegedly survive death with ego-soul intact. These die the death of Period, not the death of Act, the embodiment of vitality.

It is worthwhile pointing out ED's pioneering usage of "green" in our modern sense of "ecologically friendly." We speak of the Green Party, or of the Green Team. This latter is the American Farmland Trust, representing farmers who are environmentally aware, & honor their stewardship of the earth (e.g., organic farming). In the present poem ED refers to those who survive satori as "Green People," persons who identify human nature & Mother Nature. ED herself was obviously a "green gardener."

362

It struck me – every Day –
The Lightning was as new
As if the Cloud that instant slit
And let the Fire through –

It burned Me – in the Night –
It Blistered to My Dream –
It sickened fresh upon my sight –
With every Morn that came –

I thought that Storm – was brief –
The Maddest – quickest by –
But Nature lost the Date of This –
And left it in the Sky –

"MUCH MADNESS IS DIVINEST SENSE"

In the present poem ED identifies a period of frequent ego-transcendence in which each time seems like the first time:

> It struck me – every Day –
> The Lightning was as new
> As if the Cloud that instant slit
> And let the Fire through –

In the second stanza she says that the experience followed her at night, holding her in its grasp. Not only that,

> It sickened fresh upon my sight –
> With every Morn that came –

This is early in her career, when she suffered a distressing conflict of identity threatening madness:

> I thought that Storm – was brief –
> The Maddest – quickest by –

But even without a guru to consult she intuited that this was her true nature, & that insanity had nothing to do with her "two-mindedness." Scholars may work to "date" her poems, but ED's Nature is beyond chronology:

But Nature lost the Date of This –
And left it in the Sky –

In another early poem, P-410, she recalls her naïve fears for her sanity, & says:

That person that I was –
And this One – do not feel the same –
Could it be Madness – this?

Needless to say, that is a rhetorical question.

In P-435 she is more confident: "Much Madness is divinest Sense." In a late poem (P-1717) she calls the ego-identity an "esoteric belt" that "Protects our sanity." ("Esoteric" means "understood only by initiates"; by virtue of growing up in a given society, you are initiated into it.)

By now she takes the notion of "sanity" with a grain of salt. In ED's last years the Emily Dickinson identity existed largely to protect the ED identity.*

---

* On the theme of madness, see also P-1284 ("Had we our senses"), P-1333 ("A little Madness in the Spring"), & P-1430 ("Who never wanted – maddest Joy").

925

Struck, was I, not yet by Lightning –
Lightning – lets away
Power to perceive His Process
With Vitality.

Maimed – was I – yet not by Venture –
Stone of stolid Boy –
Nor a Sportsman's Peradventure –
Who mine Enemy?

Robbed – was I – intact to Bandit –
All my Mansion torn –
Sun – withdrawn to recognition –
Furthest shining – done –

Yet was not the foe – of any –
Not the smallest Bird
In the nearest Orchard dwelling
Best of Me – afraid.

Most – I love the Cause that slew Me.
Often as I die
Its beloved Recognition
Holds a Sun on Me –

Best – at Setting – as is Nature's –
Neither witnessed Rise
Till the infinite Aurora
In the other's eyes.

PERCEIVING THE PROCESS

This is one of ED's poems recreating the event of ego-transcendence. Enlightenment, she says, is a form of lightning, except that

> Lightning – lets away
> Power to perceive His Process
> With Vitality.

By "lets away" I understand "extinguishes," or "impairs." Any Buddhist adept will tell you that enlightenment includes the power to perceive the process.* In fact, ED's oeuvre shows her poetic power to perceive the Process, & with vitality – especially those poems that analyze it psychologically, just as Buddhist sutras do.

In the second stanza ED says that she was "maimed" – "yet not by Venture." Ego-transcendence does indeed "maim" you, because it destroys your acceptance of ego as a legitimate part of who you are; on the other hand, satori comes unexpectedly. It is not a "Venture," a risky undertaking, because you didn't undertake anything.

After satori your previous ego-self seems to have been "Stone of stolid Boy." It was set in its ways; who could have suspected such a radical change of heart?

Nor was it a sportsman's accidental injury (she goes on to say), for no opponent was involved.

---

* ED says "His Process." She regularly thinks of enlightenment as an act of the "Master," or of "God."

Stanza 3. She was "robbed... intact to Bandit." Something (ego-identify) was taken from her without her ready consent, & yet she remained intact — became intact, as a matter of fact. Enlightenment will steal your ego-self away; like a highwayman it says, "Stand & deliver!" Now ED no longer recognizes the old, ego-dominant reality that used to be "plain as day."

Stanza 4 could have been written by St. Francis. Somewhere Thoreau says similarly that birds would perch on his hat.

Stanza 5 thanks the new sun that "slew" her. Every time this happens ("Often as I die") she basks in the warmth of "Its beloved Recognition."

Stanza 6. As we in the Southwest know, this Sun is "Best at Setting." "Neither" means 1) Buddha Mind, & 2) Nature. The Sun is best at setting, when its beauty prepares you to witness its rising in the morning. After satori you realize that you are fully prepared to expect a recurrence. This brings a fullness to life that the egocentric person does not suspect. When satori recedes, it is like the sun setting: you feel that it must recur, when you will look into the eyes of the infinite Aurora. This is the upside; the downside is the fear that it will not recur — known as the Dark Night of the Soul.

315

He fumbles at your Soul
As Players at the Keys
Before they drop full Music on –
He stuns you by degrees –
Prepares you brittle Nature
For the Ethereal Blow
By fainter Hammers – further heard –
Then nearer – Then so slow
Your Breath has time to straighten –
Your Brain – to bubble Cool –
Deals – One – imperial – Thunderbolt –
That scalps your naked Soul –
When Winds take Forests in their Paws –
The Universe – is still –

Here ED endeavors to describe the experience of satori, as she will continue to do throughout her career. She relates the experience in the present tense, suggesting that it has occurred often enough for her to hazard a generalization. The opening lines suggest an orchestra tuning up, or musicians warming up:

> He fumbles at your Soul
> As Players at the Keys
> Before they drop full Music on –

This musical metaphor evokes also a performance by keyboard musicians playing in concert ("Hammers"). As you gradually feel the aura of the approaching "Ethereal Blow," you become aware of a massive buildup leading to an explosive orgasm of ego-transcendence, as depicted in the remarkable lines of P-1495:

> The Thrill came slowly like a Boon for
> Centuries delayed
> Its fitness flowing like the Flood
> In sumptuous solitude –

In line 5 ED refers to the ego-self as our "brittle Nature," meaning "rigid," "unbending"; at the same time satori demonstrates that the recalcitrant ego-self, being "brittle," is easily broken, even though it seems otherwise to meditators frustrated by years of patiently facing a blank wall.

In the last two lines ED turns from metaphoric lightning to metaphoric wind:

> When Winds take Forests in their Paws –
> The Universe – is still –

Wind is <u>Spiritus</u>, the Breath of Life. The "outer" Wind & the "inner" Wind are ultimately identical, as all meditators recognize who practice breathing meditation.

Transcendent awareness is "Still," as at the eye of the Storm of ego-consciousness. It is the archetypal stillness depicted in all the images of the Buddha, the stillness of the enlightened mind, as the storm of samsara —"history"—rages all about. The Thunderbolt of satori overrules the storm of ego-affairs.

739

I many times thought Peace had come
When Peace was far away –
As Wrecked Men – deem they sight the Land –
At Centre of the Sea –

And struggle slacker – but to prove
As hopelessly as I –
How many the fictitious Shores –
Before the Harbor be –

SHIPWRECKED

When ED speaks of "Peace," as she does here, I believe she refers
to the possibility of reconciling her secret life & her outward life:
ED & Emily Dickinson. There was always this "civil war" being
waged, as she says in P-594:

> The Battle fought between the Soul
> And No Man – is the One
> Of all the Battles prevalent –
> By far the Greater One –

P-642, cited in the prologue "The Witness Who Explains," is
the locus classicus describing her civil war, & every commentator
ought to know it by heart:

> Me from Myself – to banish –
> Had I Art –
> Impregnable my Fortress
> Unto All Heart –
>
> But since Myself – assault Me –
> How have I peace
> Except by subjugating
> Consciousness?

And since We're mutual Monarch
How this be
Except by Abdication –
Me – of Me?

Again, in P-458 ("Like Eyes that looked on Wastes"), she echoes
to the looking-glass poem (351), saying that her mirror image

So looked the face I looked upon –
So looked itself – on Me –

And then she comes to her usual tentative conclusion:

Neither – would be absolved –
Neither would be a Queen
Without the Other – Therefore –
We perish – tho' We reign –

All the above sets the scene as it were for the present poem:

I many times thought Peace had come
When Peace was far way –
As Wrecked Men – deem they sight the Land –
At Centre of the Sea –

ED's reference here to "Wrecked Men" evokes her recollection of
early satori as a traumatic event, "shattering her with Dawn" (P-323).
It was "A Crash without a Sound" (P-1581). It left her "Wrecked,
solitary, here" (P-280). Again, in P-1123, she says of satori,

A great Hope fell
You heard no noise
The Ruin was within
Oh cunning wreck that told no tale
And let no Witness in

In the present poem ED's metaphor of Wrecked Men finds them "At Centre of the Sea." This, appropriately enough, exactly describes oceanic consciousness. Satori sweeps away entirely the ego-world, the dualistic ("I/it") ontology — hence the epigram of P-1512:

> All things swept sole away
> This — is immensity —

In the second stanza of the present poem ED voices her growing realization that the "civil war" will no doubt always be a part of who she is. The Wrecked Men "deem they sight the Land,"

> And struggle slacker — but to prove
> As hopelessly as I —
> How many the fictitious Shores —
> Before the Harbor be —

This remained her besetting problem. Her family & friends could never know that Emily was also ED, nor why, as she says in P-1410:

> I shall not murmur if at last
> The ones I loved below
> Permission have to understand
> For what I shunned them so —
> Divulging it would rest my Heart
> But it would ravage theirs —

Try as she might, any given way of dealing with the alienation would always turn out to be a mirage, a "fictitious Shore," with no Harbor in sight.

1113

There is a strength in proving that it can be borne
Although it tear –
What are the sinews of such cordage for
Except to bear
The ship might be of satin had it not to fight –
To walk on seas requires cedar Feet

Ego-transcendence tears at the fabric of Psyche, i.e., the fabric woven by the society that has made us in its image. In P-278, a poem about "fair-weather friends," ED likens different "souls" (people) to different fabrics:

> The Vane a little to the East –
> Scares Muslin souls – away –
> If Broadcloth Hearts are firmer –
> Than those of Organdy –
>
> Who is to blame? The Weaver?
> Ah, the bewildering thread!

The "thread" of this poem becomes the "cordage" of P-1113, "There is a strength..." ED thinks of herself not as "thread," but as cordage, part of the rigging of a seagoing vessel.

Ego-transcendence can be difficult to be "borne," especially when it occurs in a cultural vacuum, without benefit of training, or expectations (as in a Buddhist sangha, or community*). It can easily be interpreted as a form of madness, as ED herself attests in P-410, where she says that she was "grateful that a thing / So terrible – had been endured." In the present poem she feels the "strength in proving that it can be borne."

The socialization of each person creates a split in the Psyche, consisting of ego & the "subconscious" mind (to use Freud's term). Freud himself was an egocentric thinker who tended to see ego-transcendence as a form of infantilism, a return to the womb. Transcendentalism —especially as in Buddhism—consists in restoring unity to a split Psyche. One learns to "think with the heart." This is what Jung called the Individuation Process.

---

* The three Jewels of Buddhism are Buddha, Dharma, & Sangha. The Sangha shares collectively the goal of ego-transcendence, a thing unheard of in a nineteenth-century New England community.

ED thinks of herself as a seagoing vessel made to bear the stress of adventure on the high seas of spiritual transformation. In P-401 she portrays the gentlewomen of society as made of dimity & plush. As she says of herself in the present poem, "The ship might be of satin had it not to fight." As a transcendentalist she understands that she was made to "fight" — to fight resistance to her rejection of ego. Unlike Christ, she doesn't walk on water. She walks on her sea legs, at one with the cordage & timber of the Psyche that is herself.

997

Crumbling is not an instant's Act
A fundamental pause
Dilapidation's processes
Are organized Decays.

'Tis first a Cobweb on the Soul
A Cuticle of Dust
A Borer in the Axis
An elemental Rust –

Ruin is formal – Devil's work
Consecutive & slow –
Fail in an instant, no man did
Slipping – is Crash's law.

FIRST THE SHATTERING, THEN THE CRUMBLING

The psychological meaning of "Crumbling" is given explicitly in P-1499:

> How firm Eternity must look
> To crumbling men like me
> The only Adamant Estate
> In all Identity –

The reference is to unstable ego-identity, which begins to "crumble" in the face of Eternity, the non-ego identity of satori.* ED uses "crumble" because of its inchoative force. It means <u>gradual</u> disintegration. Ego-transcendence, as an episode, can initiate the crumbling of the ego-self, but this process involves a lifetime of individuating, as ED knows, speaking from her own experience:

> Crumbling is not an instant's Act
> A fundamental pause
> Dilapidation's processes
> Are organized Decays.

---

* This poem is discussed in <u>Accidental Buddhist,</u> pp   , where it is illustrated with the Zen koan, "What was your original face, the one you had before your parents were born?"

An episode of satori is "A fundamental pause." This is a striking description, evoking P-1295, where ED says of satori,

> Eternity will be
> Velocity or Pause
> At Fundamental Signals
> From Fundamental Laws

And so a series of transcendent episodes over time can appear as "organized Decays" — "organized," because they are organic, affecting the very structure of Psyche.

In the second stanza ED applies the housekeeping metaphor to the House of Psyche:

> 'Tis first a Cobweb on the Soul
> A Cuticle of Dust
> A Borer in the Axis
> An Elemental Rust —

The "Axis" being bored is the <u>axis mundi,</u> the egocentric axis, or worldview, around which one's daily life revolves. Buddha Mind functions as a "Borer in the Axis," impeding the function of the ego-self. After satori, there is no more "Fairy Oil" (P-983) to lubricate our conventional worldview, & so it begins to rust.

Stanza three contrasts "Crumbling" & "Ruin":

> Ruin is formal — Devil's work
> Consecutive & slow —
> Fail in an instant, no man did
> Slipping — is Crash's law.

I take "formal ruin" to mean the slow disintegration of the outward form, whether of the Parthenon, or of my own aging body. The psychological crumbling occasioned by ego-transcendence, however is not "formal." It does not pertain to the look of things; it is "Devil's work," says ED the heretic, knowing full well that she had best keep hidden her stash of unchristian sutras. Individuation −the slow crumbling of the ego-identity—is "Consecutive & slow." No one "instant" or "pause" can make you fail to appear outwardly any different; but "Slipping − is Crash's law."

"Crash" is satori, the momentary collapse of the ego-self, as in P-1503, where it is described as "The Crash of nothing yet of all," or in P-1581, "A Crash without a Sound." The sudden crash of ego, if only for a moment, puts you on a slippery slope, for "Slipping − is Crash's law."

1123

A great Hope fell
You heard no noise
The Ruin was within
Oh cunning wreck that told no tale
And let no Witness in

The mind was built for mighty Freight
For dread occasion planned
How often foundering at Sea
Ostensibly, on Land

A not admitting of the wound
Until it grew so wide
That all my Life had entered it
And there were troughs beside

A closing of the simple lid
That opened to the sun
Until the tender carpenter
Perpetual nail it down -

THE WIDENING WOUND

Satori may seem like a great electric storm in the mind, but eerily it is a silent event, "A crash without a Sound" (P-1581). In the present poem ED describes satori as a silent wreck:

> A great Hope fell
> You heard no noise
> The Ruin was within
> Oh cunning wreck that told no tale
> And let no Witness in

Motifs of the individuation struggle are addressed in this poem, even as it focuses specifically on loss of belief in the Christian myth. The opening line refers to the world of the illusory ego-self as belief in the New Testament ("Hope"), the promise of life after death through Jesus Christ.

The silent, unwitnessed fall of the "great Hope" demonstrates the unexpected powers of the liberated mind:

> The mind was built for mighty Freight
> For dread occasion planned

Ego regards satori as a "dread occasion" (Its own demise), & socialization seems to be planned that way. From childhood on our everyday awareness is programmed to see the ego-self as the basic reality, & is primed to reject death as the demise of ego. It learns to see death as the gateway to Heaven. This being the case, satori may be rationalized as temporary insanity, rather than revelation of truth.

But ED recognizes that her acceptance of ego-death is inevitable, because it frees one to take on the "mighty freight" that the mind is meant to carry. In P-1225 this "Freight" appears as the substance of the creative unconscious:

> Its Hour with itself
> The Spirit never shows.
> What Terror would enthrall the Street
> Could Countenance disclose
>
> The Subterranean Freight
> The Cellars of the Soul –

Line 8 of the present poem begins a statement that continues into the following stanza:

> How often foundering at Sea
> Ostensibly, on Land
>
> A not admitting of the wound
> Until it grew so wide
> That all my Life had entered it
> And there were troughs beside

Here ED refers to the serial episodes of satori that created an ever-widening "wound" (trauma). She describes satori as "foundering at Sea / Ostensibly, on Land." Conventional people consider the cultural ego-self to be stable ("on Land") – indeed, they simply take this for granted, without a thought. But sudden loss of the ego-reality leaves one "foundering at Sea."

In the beginning ED attempted to deny the reality of ego's

non-existence, but with further episodes of satori the wound "grew so wide" that she surrendered to the truth.

Initially this seems impossible; eventually it is inevitable. You can remain in denial only so long.

The "troughs" are part of the Sea metaphor: like a transcendental surfer ED went with the crest of the breaker.

The final stanza makes an unexpectedly tender reference to her loss of faith in the Christian myth:

> A closing of the simple lid
> That opened to the sun
> Until the tender carpenter
> Perpetual nail it down –

To lose faith in Christianity is to lose faith in Jesus Christ. Jesus was an enlightened carpenter, as Dickinson was an enlightened householder. When you accept this view of Christ, the "tender Carpenter" will drive the final nail into coffin lid – the lid that supposedly opened like a door to the resurrection of ego.

1490

The Face in evanescence lain
Is more distinct than ours –
And ours surrendered for its sake
As Capsules are for Flower's
Or is it the confiding sheen
Dissenting to be won
Descending to enamor us
Of Detriment divine?

To be a Flower, is profound
Responsibility –

(From P-1058)

DETRIMENT DIVINE

Central to the experience of satori is one's sense of reality as impermanent, beginning with one's own ego-self. The Buddhist term for impermanence is <u>anicca,</u> by which is meant not simply the obvious understanding that everything passes away, like the snows of yesteryear, but that the "things" of "everything" have no self-hood, just as the rainbow has no selfhood; it is all a mirage.

ED knows anicca by personal experience, & in the present poem she indicates this by her reference to the inchoative verb "evanesce":

> The Face in evanescence lain
> Is more distinct than ours –

The world reality itself is inchoative, a flux of evanescence, the human face being our most obvious example. When one dies, the face is frozen "in evanescence," evanescence being its fluid, ever-changing mode of existence.

The face of a corpse "Is more distinct than ours," says ED, with a touch of irony, for this is precisely the paradox revealed by anicca. We regard the everyday, egocentric reality (samsara) as "distinct" –the tree, the house, the cow—because it is a static concept, an abstraction. Divorced from the flux of reality, it is a dead thing, like a rainbow silkscreened on a T-shirt. We believe that our own ego-self is an entity that can survive death & live eternally as an "ego-soul." Theologians may argue the point, but the churchgoers make no bones about it: without survival of the ego-self, an "afterlife" loses meaning. So samsara is chock-full of "distinct" realities. With satori, they vanish, like the "things" painted on a scrim curtain suddenly backlighted.

The idea presented in lines 1-2 of the present poem is developed in lines 3-4:

> The Face in evanescence lain
> Is more distinct than ours –
> And ours surrendered for its sake
> As Capsules are for Flower's –

I take "it" ("its sake") as referring to death – meaning both actual death, & the ego-death of satori. In either case we surrender the "distinct" fact of reality for the evanescent reality of anicca, the world of unconditioned awareness, or Buddha Mind.

ED develops this thought with a simile, "As Capsules are for Flower's." "Capsule" means "spore sac," or "seedpod."* The apparently "distinct" face of the ego-self exists for one basic reason; to be transcended. Ego-transcendence cannot happen without ego, nor can ED exist without Dickinson. So our everyday "distinct" reality is actually a seedpod awaiting sunlight, as she says in P-1255:

---

* Cf. P-1264: "The seed of disappointment grew / Within a capsule gay." Arthur Conan Doyle (1859-1930) uses the word this way in this story, "The Naval Treaty." Sherlock Holmes says of the board-schools, "Beacons of the future! Capsules with hundreds of bright little seeds in each" [The Complete Sherlock Holmes, 456-7].

Longing is like the Seed
That wrestles in the Ground,
Believing if it intercede
It shall at length be found.

The Hour, & the Clime –
Each Circumstance unknown,
What Constancy must be achieved
Before it see the Sun!

To "see the Sun" is to experience enlightenment. To be born as a human being, with a human consciousness, implies an existential "responsibility," as stated in our epigraph:

To be a Flower, is profound
Responsibility –

So far so good. But now ED suggests that we look at the matter from the other, Higher Ground;

Or is it the confiding sheen
Dissenting to be won
Descending to enamor us
Of Detriment divine?

When you experience satori, you (like a seed in the ground), grow into a flowering consciousness, thanks to the warmth of the Sun. This experience seems like Divine Grace – here, a "confiding sheen." The Tao is "confiding" in you, taking you into its confidence.

Every serious meditator knows well that satori cannot be "won." You can court it all you like, without success, while someone else, an innocent bystander (like Dickinson) is just "chosen," as if by some cosmic lottery. It all has to do with ego

& the way it functions within the dynamic of each individual Psyche. Psyche uses dreams to keep in touch, but the Oracle is cryptic.

Satori is, first of all, Grace, experienced as a Divine Lover. The mystics have always felt this to be so, just as ED, in P-356:

> The Grace that I – was chose –
> To Me – surpassed the Crown
> That was the Witness for the Grace –
> 'Twas even that 'twas Mine –

In the present poem ED calls the Divine lover "the confiding sheen," "detrimentum, meaning "severe damage," "loss," "defeat."

She is almost certainly using "detriment" as a Latinism, detrimentum, meaning "severe damage," "loss," "defeat." Satori entails the "detriment" of ego & egocentric reality. In fact, "Detriment divine" is simply one more of ED's many coinages to describe satori.

180

As if some little Arctic flower
Upon the polar hem –
Went wandering down the Latitudes
Until it puzzled came
To continents of summer –
To firmaments of sun –
To strange, bright crowds of flowers –
And birds, of foreign tongue!
I say, As if this little flower
To Eden, wandered in –
What then? Why nothing,
Only, your inference therefrom!

"GEE, CARLO, I DON'T THINK WE'RE IN AMHERST ANYMORE."

This poem evokes the film version of L. Frank Baum's <u>Wizard of Oz</u>: the opening scenes, set in Kansas, are in black-&-white; upon Dorothy's arrival in Oz, the film switches to Technicolor. Similarly, the present poem begins "Upon the polar hem," a region of black-&-white, & then changes

> To continents of summer –
> To firmaments of sun –
> To strange, bright crowds of flowers –
> And birds, of foreign tongue!

[Non-ego awareness perceives the world as ego-consciousness has never perceived it; hence the "foreign tongue.]
    Baum's Oz is ED's Eden ("EDen," as I like to think of it). Being a "flower child" herself, ED "infers" – what?

> I say, As if this little flower
> To Eden, wandered in –
> What then? Why nothing,
> Only, your inference therefrom!

This passage is very characteristic of ED's "interactive style," where the reader is expected to recognize the subtext. It is the discourse of an oracle, hence "cryptic" to the egocentric reader, who expects to have it all spelled out in black-&-white. But ED's discourse is "esoteric," as she reminds herself in P-1452:

> Your thoughts don't have words every day
> They come a single time
> Like signal esoteric sips
> Of the communion Wine

"Esoteric" means "written for the initiated," whom she addresses in the present poem:

> What then? Why nothing,
> Only, your inference therefrom!

"To infer" means "to derive as a conclusion from the facts." If you have not experienced these facts personally, then you can infer nothing from the words of the oracle. On the other hand, if you have experienced even mild satori, or a numinous dream, you will recognize your "inference" as part of the experience; it is the affect, or emotional involvement filling your heart. With a shock of recognition, you understand that you have awakened in your natural Home on Earth: you "infer" that this is where you belong. It is what ED calls "the neighboring life: in P-159. It is the House of P-1360:

> I sued the News – yet feared – the News
> That such a Realm could be –
> "The House not made with Hands" it was –
> Thrown open wide to me –

Nature welcomes you back, like a prodigal son or daughter, into her Parlor, as ED puts it in P-304:

The Orchard sparkled like a Jewel –
How mighty 'twas – to be
A Guest in this stupendous place –
The Parlor – of the Day –

Any close reading of an ED poem, so long as it is on ED's wavelength, is an "inference therefrom."*

---

* The quote from P-304 includes the required emendation ("Jewel," not "Jew").

EMILY DICKINSON & ED: CONFLICT OF INTERESTS

When ego-transcendence occurs suddenly & unexpectedly to an innocent bystander, it may come as a psychic upheaval, & leave in its wake a conflict of identity. This is what ED describes often throughout her oeuvre. Let the following four poems serve as examples.

P-1549, "My Wars are laid away in Books." The primary "war" is, or course, the identity conflict that evolved over several decades —what I call the Thirty-five Years War, consisting of many a battle, all duly recorded as poems, & "laid away" in her self-crafted booklets.

P-364, "The Morning after Woe." This early poem describes the conflict "the Morning after," when the return from transcendence leaves a confused sense of the need to reconcile inner Nature & outer Nature.

P-351, "I felt my life with both my hands." Satori has unleashed a creative force that will not be denied, & Psyche seems to have a new "Owner," & a new "Home."

P-417, "It is dead — Find it." Dickinson is in process of recognizing the inner conditions necessary for any long-term happiness, & intuits the kind of "home-sickness" deeply felt by the transcendental temperament.

With devaluation of the old ego-self comes the felt need to embrace a dharma-centered life focused on the Higher Self, the one I call ED. The following poems document this individuating process.

P-427, "I'll clutch — & clutch." This extraordinary interior apostrophe is a passionate declaration of love, offering a vision of dharma-centered union.

P-664, "Of all the Souls that stand create." This poem declares a firm commitment to the Higher Self.

P-870, "Finding is the first Act." Here ED recognizes the Treasure Hard to Find, a solid connection with the creative unconscious.

P-33, "If recollecting were forgetting," & P-458, "Like Eyes that looked on Wastes." ED mulls over the two-in-one paradox of her divided, yet undivided identity, elsewhere called "Mutual Monarch" (P-542).

P-684, "Best Gains – must have the Losses' Test," & P-424, "Removed from Accident of Loss." These two poems concern the relativity of gain & loss: what is a gain for Dickinson is a loss for ED, & vice-versa.

1549

My Wars are laid away in Books –
I have one Battle more –
A Foe whom I have never seen
But oft has canned me o'er –
And hesitated me between
And others at my side,
But chose the best – Neglecting me – till
All the rest, have died –
How sweet if I am not forgot
By Chums that passed away –
Since Playmates at threescore & ten
Are such a scarcity -

THE THIRTY-FIVE YEARS WAR

This late poem is the one that gave Alfred Habegger the title of his biography of Dickinson, <u>My Wars Are Laid Away in Books</u>. He naturally treats it as an autobiographical reference, a "summing up" (as Sewall calls it*). It is here, he says, where Dickinson leaves the subject of love "for good." As a "definitive work of retrospection" it lets us know that love, "its pain, its play — had been completed, turned into art, & laid away in the poet's secret homemade manuscript book."**

Essential to a close reading of this poem is our understanding of the word "Wars." According to Habegger, it refers to the trials of love; Dickinson had used these as autobiographical material for her poetry, "turned love into art," & stored this in the attic as it were. Since Habegger uses the opening line as the title for his book, he gives us to understand that Dickinson's love life is the primary subject of her poetry. This idea is much too pat ("love turned into art"), not to say inadmissible, considering that ED is a transcendentalist poet probing archetypal themes raised to consciousness during some thirty-five years.

The principal "War" experienced by ED was the lifelong struggle between ego & non-ego, between Dickinson & ED, as she states clearly in P-594. We have quoted it before, & it bears quoting again:

---

*   <u>Life</u>, 699.

** 600-1

The Battle fought between the Soul
And No Man – is the One
Of all the Battles prevalent –
By far the Greater One –

No News of it is had abroad –
Its Bodiless Campaign
Establishes, & terminates –
Invisible – Unknown –

This poem, dated 1862, was written during the War Between the States; so it is natural that she would see her own inner strife as a Civil War, here & in other equally unequivocal poems (e.g., 340, 446, 458, 642, 683).

This thirty-five year war entailed many battles, not the least of which was that one regarding "Chums" & "Playmates" (lines 10-11). These terms, belonging to childhood, place adult relationships in their proper perspectives, from the transcendentalist viewpoint: ego-attachment to other people is immature, so long as it prevents further individuating, so long as it remains a hang-up.

This poem, written in her last years, reflects the monastic life that she had come to adopt. Now, in her fifties, she recognizes the three decades of creative effort grounded in the inner war that has always been a significant source of inspiration. She became alienated from human attachments. She came to see these as milestones along her Path to the Higher Self. This was painful & traumatic, & each poem became a war that she laid away—secreted—as privileged information regarding the recesses of her heart.

ED died at the age of fifty-six. In the present poem she suggests that she is seventy: "threescore & ten." This is the common human lifespan, according to the Bible (Psalms 90:10); so ED appears to be using this to mean that she has fulfilled her vocation, that she has, in effect, accomplished by now what she was put on earth to do. Nonetheless, I am inclined to see a further hind of meaning in this biblical reference. Psalms 90:10 tells us that "The days of our years are threescore & ten"; but in the verse immediately preceding we read, "We spend our years as a tale that is told." By age fifty ED was certainly aware that she had spent her years "as a tale that is told": what is her body of poetry, if not that?

364

The Morning after Woe –
'Tis frequently the Way –
Surpasses all that rose before –
For utter Jubilee –

As Nature did not care –
And piled her Blossoms on –
And further to parade a Joy
Her Victim stared upon –

The Birds declaim their Tunes –
Pronouncing every word
Like Hammers – Did they know they fell
Like Litanies of Lead –

On here & there – a creature –
They'd modify the Glee
To fit some Crucifixal Clef –
Some Key of Calvary -

THE MORNING AFTER: A CRUCIFIXAL CLEF

This poem appears to be a philosophical reflection on some unhappy event, or events in Dickinson's life, & the aftermath. The "Woe" could well be the death of someone close. If this is indeed the case, then we must see how ED's unique viewpoint compares with the conventional one, for she always brings to bear a complex perspective, given the sophistication of her own inner life. Her inner life crucially affects her outer life. Like most deep people ED is not readily the emotional victim of circumstances.

"Woe" may be of two kinds, egocentric or ego-transcendent. The former is the "Suffering" (duhkha) recognized by the Buddhists' First Noble Truth: Life is suffering; or, as ED puts it in P-1168,

> As old as Woe —
> How old is that?
> Some eighteen thousand years —

Transcendental woe is the deep depression known as the Dark Night of the Soul, when, after satori, you "come down" & begin to sense the acute sorrow of separation. The depth of the "down" no doubt reflects the degree of the "high." It is as if you had met your soulmate, fallen madly in love — only to have your soulmate disappear without explanation, perhaps forever. ED experienced this a number of times, as her poetry attests, causing her commentators no end of speculation concerning her outer, everyday life. In P-256 she calls herself "banished"; in P-477 the

Separation Anxiety is called "Despair"; in P-770, it is "Dread"; in P-1580, "dismay" [at "Old Suitor Heaven"].

"Woe," in the context of the present poem, is this same Dread, as clearly is dictated by the detailed description. In the opening lines ED makes what seems to be a debatable generalization:

> The Morning after Woe –
> 'Tis frequently the Way –
> Surpasses all that rose before –
> For utter Jubilee –

One must ask whether what ED says here "frequently" happens. "Woe" is an inner tragedy, a deep sorrow, as at the death of a loved one; "Jubilee" here refers to Mother Nature celebrating springtime; we suffer a profound woe – & awaken to a joyous spring morning. Why should ED say that this "frequently" happens, as if any reader would readily recognize such a fact, once it is pointed out?

But that is surely a non-problem, since ED is speaking of her own inner experience. Only she can say whether it is "frequent" or not. Such is the case in P-1452 ("Your thoughts don't have words every day"), where she speaks of the frequency of her poetic inspiration. There she tells herself,

> You cannot comprehend its price
> Nor its infrequency

In the present poem ED establishes a Woe/Jubilee dialectic. The joy of satori is readily experienced as a "Jubilee" – exhilaration, ecstasy, rapture, etc., & this is a happiness felt by Psyche, Mother Nature in human form. What we are getting at here [ED & I] is that Nature's inner jubilee is "frequently" followed by the woe of separation: it reappears in Nature's outer Jubilee, regardless of the season of the year. ED visualizes this sharply:

> As Nature did not care –
> And piled her Blossoms on –
> And further to parade a Joy
> Her Victim stared upon –

ED herself is the "Victim" staring at the riot of springtime, for she seems to have been banished, or exiled, from the dharma, so acute is her grief. The songbirds seem to mock her alienation; they "declaim their Tunes - / Pronouncing every word / Like Hammer." If these birds knew that their "Litanies of Lead" fell

> On here & there – a creature –
> They'd modify the Glee
> To fit some Crucifixal Clef –
> Some Key of Calvary –

In her discourse, ED uses "Calvary" bimodally, i.e., in the egocentric mode & in the ego-transcendent mode. In P-1072 ("Title divine – is mine!") she calls herself "Empress of Calvary!" It is a divine Title "conferred" on her:

> Title divine – is mine!
> The wife – without the Sign!
> Acute Degree – conferred on me –
> Empress of Calvary!

This archetypal use of "Calvary" means the sacrifice of a specific human ego-self, thereby revealing the Divine Self. Satori means (momentary) death of little self, unveiling Great Self, like a scrim curtain suddenly backlighted.

In the present poem "Calvary" is used in the egocentric

mode. Calvary is always a <u>sacrifice</u>, regardless of mode. In the Dark Night of the Soul —a deep depression—the sufferer senses only that his or her spiritual well-being, the sense of Oneness or Centeredness, has been cruelly sacrificed. It is here that ED creates one of her many inspired coinages: "Crucifixal Clef." This is one way to describe the Dark Night of the Soul. The Song of the Earth is now perceived as a dirge. "Clef" may well have occurred to ED by reason of its similarity to the word "cleft," meaning a split, or shattering.

351

I felt my life with both my hands
To see if it was there –
I held my spirit to the Glass,
To prove it possibler –

I turned my Being round & round
And paused at every pound
To ask the Owner's name –
For doubt, that I should know the Sound –

I judged my features – jarred my hair –
I pushed my dimples by & waited –
If they – twinkled back –
Conviction might, of me –

I told myself, "Take Courage, Friend –
That – was a former time –
But we might learn to like the Heaven,
As well as our Old Home!"

CONFLICTING IMAGES

In the present poem —an early one at that—ED has already begun to deal with the question of her personal identity. Like every other transcendentalist, she will mull over this question throughout life.

This question is not a "psychological problem," but rather a psychological challenge. By this I mean a challenge from Psyche. One can identify selfhood with ego, or with Psyche. If the latter, you fly free; if the former, you sentence yourself to life imprisonment.

Early on, Emily Dickinson determined to create a dual lifestyle wherein she, as witness/poet, would celebrate & commemorate her experiences as Buddha Mind. She stayed the course for 35 years of dedicated creativity until the day she was "called back."

The present poem is one of her most autobiographical ones, similar to P-563, where the last stanza says,

> I do not doubt the self I was
> Was competent to me –
> But something awkward in the fit –
> Proves that – outgrown – I see –

The dual life shared by Emily Dickinson & ED reminds me of the changing phases of the moon, where the shining crescent symbolizes ED.* The present poem is a full statement central to

---

* See P-629 & P-737 for a detailed portrait of the moon as the Higher Self.

the challenge of a duality that seesaws between ego-dominance & ego-transcendence.

I call this type of transcendentalist poem a "sutra," because it, like the traditional Buddhist sutras, is a terse statement about Selfhood. The ED sutra is psychologically astute & clearheaded —even analytical—rather than warmly emotional, like a Chopin prelude.

The challenge of questioning one's selfhood certainly stirs deep emotion, but ED does not make this part of her poetic voice. I never allow myself to forget that ED was alone in Amherst, like a closeted gay. She was alone & she didn't panic. That's why she knew it was necessary to stay calm, & to keep it together. Emily Dickinson lived among family & friends, but ED was the Stranger in Town, welcomed only by one person: Emily Dickinson. Thanks to Dickinson's intelligent, unending hospitality, we have this book of poems. It would have been easy to panic; she said, "Hold on, this is what we're going to do."

These very poems are living evidence of ED's hospitality, & also Emily Dickinson's hospitality. ED, with her knowledge of Latin, knew very well that "Host" & "Guest" are cognate, both from L. hospes (see P-674 & P-1721). So, in the world of Psyche, who is the guest, & who is the host? In the present poem ED says that she mulled over & over the question of selfhood, "To ask the Owner's name." She examines her face in the mirror & talks to her image. Most of us are unwilling to confront the ego-identity; we accept it uncritically. But ED insists upon a confrontation, as she states most forcefully in the third stanza:

> I judged my features – jarred my hair –
> I pushed my dimples by, & waited –
> If they – twinkled back –
> Conviction might, or me –

Here she opts for an open-ended syntax, with a predicate to be inferred by the interactive reader. I infer as follows: "I waited to see if conviction of me might occur." Her use of "conviction" relies upon the double meaning of this word: (1) "The act or process of convicting of a crime," & (2) "The act of convincing a person of error or of compelling the admission of a truth" (Merriam-Webster).

Everyone has a "self-image"; Buddhist practice (meditation) consists in changing the self-identity from ego to non-ego. Through meditation you liberate the Self from the illusion that the ego-self has an inherent existence. ED, contemplating her mirror image, knows that two understandings are possible: (1) she can "convict" her ego-self of ontological fraud —a spiritual crime, as it were— & (2) she can convince herself of her error & compel an admission of truth. "Emily Dickinson" is an ontological error; ED is the truth. This dynamic goes on in the mind of the serious meditator; in the present poem ED herself is meditating before a mirror.

Lama Yeshe (1935-84), "teacher of hippies," taught young Americans that meditation was a form of "talking to yourself." People become confused & unhappy, he wrote,

> through their inability to examine their own mind. They cannot explain themselves to themselves; they don't know how to talk to themselves. ... They are ignorant of their internal world, & their minds are totally unified with ignorance instead of being awake... Examine your own mental attitudes. Become your own therapist.*

This statement interests me especially, because ED's oeuvre is, among other things, a continual "talking to herself," refusing to

---

* <u>Tricycle</u> (Summer, 2000), 30.

be "unified with ignorance." This is especially true of the last stanza, where ED assures Emily Dickinson that her sense of self "was a former time," before satori. The ego-self she grew up with was her "Old Home," & the alien non-ego identity takes some getting used to; so try it, you'll like it.

417

It is dead – Find it –
Out of sound – Out of sight –
"Happy"? Which is wiser –
You, or the wind?
"Conscious"? Won't you ask that –
Of the low Ground?

"Homesick"? Many met it –
Even through them – This
Cannot testify –
Themself – as dumb –

HARMONY FROM CONFLICT

Throughout her poetry ED returns repeatedly to three themes, or issues, of utmost importance to her well-being: 1) her sense of personal fulfillment, 2) her sense of vital awareness, & 3) her sense of living at the center of a reality larger than anything her domestic circumstances could offer. In the present terse poem she epitomizes these issues in three words: "Happy," "Conscious," "Homesick."

This is one of ED's many "It" poems concerning satori. She experienced episodes of ego-transcendence throughout her life, & in between these episodes she resumed her everyday life as an enlightened ego-self, bereft of Buddha Mind. It is a great mystery how Buddha Mind can be fully, immensely present, only to disappear like a dream lost beyond recall. One may mimic it with drugs, just as one may mimic love with masturbation; indeed, in P-393 ED critiques the drug-inspired high:

> Did Our Best Moment last –
> 'Twould supersede the Heaven –
> A few – & they by Risk – procure –
> So this Sort – are not given –
>
> Except as stimulants – in
> Case of Despair –

The realized transcendentalist, between highs, lives in the dharma, ever aware of samsara, the secular world, as an illusion, never forgetting the mysterious absence of the Absolute Reality:

> It is dead – Find it –
> Out of sound – Out of sight –

Transcendentalists universally recognize the two contrasting states of awareness, egocentric & ego-transcendent. But there is also an intermediate state to be considered, the egocentric state of the realized individual. Such a one lives daily in the dharma, guided by an awakened ego. If conventional, secular people are "egocentric," then perhaps we may call the veteran transcendentalist "dharma-centric." They may be priests or nuns; they may be lay creative people, artists & poets; they may also be any introspective person living privately in tune with a special habitat. Traditional tribal people who keep the faith & the wisdom of the elders are dharma-centric without a doubt. It is a matter of living beyond the narrow limitations of the collective, secular ego & its obsession with goals & competition.

As a dharma-centric person ED was aware of the three states of consciousness we have been describing, as is evident throughout her oeuvre. This is especially so in the present poem, where she considers three characteristics of everyday consciousness especially important to her: "happy," "conscious," & "homesick."

The meaning of "happiness" is so relative that it seems to be a useless term. ED with her accustomed skepticism, asks,

> "Happy? Which is wiser –
> You, or the Wind?

Any natural phenomenon can be said to be "happy," in the sense of "careless," "without cares," as the stone of P-1510:

> How happy is the little Stone
> That rambles in the Road alone,
> And doesn't care about Careers
> And Exigencies never fears –

This is non-ego happiness. There is no conscious ego-self to worry about anything. In this sense, "happiness" is equated with the wisdom of non-ego; as the Zen saying has it, "In Nature, nobody is doing anything; yet everything gets done." If the dharma-centric ED is "happy," it is because there is an ego-self to enjoy her happiness. This is, however, qualitatively different from the bliss of ego-extinction, where consciousness is Spiritus/ Wind.

How about "Conscious"?

> "Conscious"? Won't you ask that –
> Of the low Ground?

As a dharma-centric person ED experiences a higher consciousness – but what is this, compared to non-ego awareness? Her use here of the expression "low Ground" reappears in P-1234, where she says,

> Mortality's Ground Floor
> Is Immortality –

This is the Ground of Reality, the ultimate criterion of "consciousness."

What about "Homesick"? "Home" is a special theme in the poetry of ED, for every human being has two homes: our original home in the bosom of Nature (Eden), & our secular home where we grew up, our hometown.

In P-167 ED comes to grips with the two kinds of homesickness, egocentric & ego-transcendent:

> To learn the Transport by the Pain –
> As blind Men learn the sun!
> To die of thirst – suspecting
> That Brooks in Meadows run!

This refers to one's secret intuition that "home" is not one's hometown:

> To stay the homesick – homesick feet
> Upon a foreign shore –
> Haunted by native lands, the while –
> And blue – beloved air!

Here the "foreign shore" is one's very hometown, the place where one was born & reared. But your place of birth is contingent, & cannot make you forget your original home: "This is the Sovereign Anguish!" she says:

> This is the Sovereign Anguish!
> This – the signal woe!

The Sovereign Anguish rules ED's poetry. Her poetry is the echo produced by all transcendentalist poets:

> These are the patient "Laureates"
> Whose voices – trained – below –
>
> Ascend in ceaseless Carol –
> Inaudible, indeed,
> To us – the duller scholars
> Of the Mysterious Bard!

In the present poem ED recognizes that there are many dharma-centric persons without the gift to create poetry — they are dumb:

> "Homesick"? Many met it —
> Even through them — This
> Cannot testify —
> Themselves — as dumb —

ED herself is not dumb, & has been called to testify. She testifies to the truth of dharma-centrism. She is at once Dickinson & ED. She is at once happy & unhappy, conscious & unconscious, homesick & comfortably at home. This is a major awareness alive throughout her life.

427

I'll clutch – & clutch –
Next – One – Might be the golden touch –
Could take it –
Diamonds – Wait –
I'm diving – just a little late –
But stars – go slow – for night –

I'll string you – in fine Necklace –
Tiaras – make – of some –
Wear you on Hem –
Loop up a Countess – with you –
Make – a Diadem – & mend my old One –
Count – Hoard – then lose –
And doubt that you are mine –
To have the joy of feeling it – again –

I'll show you at the Court –
Bear you – for Ornament
Where Women breathe –
That every sigh – may lift you
Just as high – as I –

And – when I die –
In meek array - display you –
Still to show – how rich I go –
Lest Skies impeach a wealth so wonderful –
And banish me -

SUING FOR PEACE

This poem is the most elaborate of ED's interior dialogues between the Higher Self & the ego-self. Some of these are tersely straightforward, clearly addressing the duality ED/Emily Dickinson, as P-642 ("Me from Myself – to banish"), or P-446, where the Higher Self is the narrator, recalling Dickinson's reticence to abandon herself to the dharma:

> I showed her Heights she never saw –
> "Would'st Climb," I said?
> She said – "Not so" –
> "With *me* – " I said – With *me*?

P-683 allows that the ego-self may regard the Higher Self both as an "imperial friend," & as an enemy agent seeking to destroy the conventional self living in samsara:

> The Soul unto itself
> Is an imperial friend –
> Or the most agonizing Spy –
> An Enemy – could send –

"Imperial friend" should be compared with the "imperial few" (the transcendentalists) of P-1577:

Morning is due to all –
To some – the Night –
To an imperial few –
The Auroral light.

The present poem reads like an extravagant marriage proposal, full of expansive, hyperbolic promises. ED is wooing Dickinson, out of the frantic need to keep fat hold on the unique opportunity to enter the dharma, & devil take the hindmost:

I'll clutch – & clutch –
Next – One – Might be the golden touch –
Could take it –

There follows a litany detailing rebirth into the nobility & plenitude of the dharma, characteristic of ED's discourse: the ego-self is a commoner & Buddha Mind is royalty/nobility – Queen (P-493), King (P-1176), Majesty (P-290), Prince (P-959) – & satori is a coronation (P-356).

In the present poem ED describes a special kind of joy familiar to many realized transcendentalists, the ones who have experienced satori at least twice:

Make – a Diadem – & mend my old One –
Count – Hoard – then lose –
And doubt that you are mine –
To have the joy of feeling it – again –

Until one is "actualized" –irreversibly absorbed into the dharma identity—one drifts in & out, sometimes haunted by the fear that "It" has forsaken one; such is the dark night of the soul. But then, unaccountably, "It" returns, & you "have the joy of feeling it – again."

In lines 15-17 ED promises to honor the ego-self:

> I'll show you at the Court –
> Bear you – for Ornament
> Where women breathe –

That is to say, the image of the ego-self will be treasured as in a locket worn on the breast, "Where Women breathe." Incorporation of the ego-self into the dharma does not mean "self-destruction." The ego-self is always honored, for it is the means whereby ego-transcendence is made possible. One unites with the Spirit, the Breath of Life – & in so doing, wears a locket on the breast, "Where Women breathe." ED recognizes the one who made it possible.

For me, the closing lines (20-24) inevitably describe ED's bequest to us, her heirs. We hold this in our hands, the "meek array" of poems written in a frugal style, bearing witness to "how rich" she went:

> And – when I die –
> In meek array – display you –
> Still to show – how rich I go –
> Lest Skies impeach a wealth so wonderful –
> And banish me –

ED understood satori as the awakening of her poetic voice, as she says in P-1554:

> "Go tell it" – What a Message –
> To whom – is specified –
> Not murmur – not endearment –
> But simply – we –obeyed –

In the present poem she calls satori "a wealth so wonderful" (line 23), recalling the unforgettable P-323:

> As if I asked a common Alms,
> And in my wondering hand
> A Stranger pressed a Kingdom,
> And I, bewildered, stand –

She recognized her Calling as an existential imperative. The dharma was her natural habitat, but on condition that she be witness/poet. This is what kept her there; otherwise she would perforce banish herself.

664

Of all the Souls that stand create –
I have elected – One –
When Sense from Spirit – files away –
And Subterfuge – is done –
When that which is – & that which was –
Apart – intrinsic – stand –
And this brief Drama in the flesh –
Is shifted – like a Sand –
When Figures show their royal Front –
And Mists – are carved away,
Behold the Atom – I preferred –
To all the lists of Clay!

COMMITMENT TO HARMONY

The "civil war" (P-594) between Dickinson & ED became a life long struggle (poems 446, 458, 642), though gradually ED came to dominate as the reclusive Woman in White, a de facto monastic. In P-340 this conflict appears in the form of foot/shoe, where, facing a patch of mud in the street, Dickinson asks,

> Is Bliss then, such Abyss,
> I must not put my foot amiss
> For fear I spoil my shoe?

She ruefully concludes that Dickinson wins out on this occasion:

> Say, Foot, decide the point –
> The Lady cross, or not?
> Verdict for Boot!

The present poem is written in the spirit of self-confidence —or Self-confidence—& the desire to commit to the transcendent reality of the Higher Self:

> Of all the Souls that stand create –
> I have elected – One –

ED proceeds to recognize the impermanence of all aspects of identity associated with the ego-self, speaking of physical death as the final arbiter:

When Sense from Spirit – files away –
And Subterfuge – is done –
When that which is – & that which was –
Apart – intrinsic – stand –

We should recognize immediately that the basis for this conflict between Dickinson & ED is ego-transcendence, which is discovered to be a dress rehearsal for physical death. Satori separates "Sense from Spirit," because the Tao is ineffable & cannot be grasped by ego-intellect: it does not yield to "sense." It reveals the cultural ego-identity, contingent upon time & place, to be a "Subterfuge." A subterfuge (from L. –fugere, "to flee") is an artifice to escape or evade the truth of its own impermanence.

Lines 5-6 define clearly the experience of non-ego awareness:

When that which is – & that which was –
Apart – intrinsic – stand –

Satori reveals ego as "that which was." It has briefly dissolved, & cosmic awareness is "that which is."

Lines 7-8 state the "transvaluation of values" created by satori:

And this brief Drama in the flesh –
Is shifted – like a Sand –

Each human life is a "brief Drama in the flesh," of course – but so is an episode of satori. Satori reveals life in a nutshell; it is an occurrence

When Figures show their royal Front –
And Mists – are carved away,

128

We have noted how ED often refers to Buddha Mind in terms of royalty; in the present poem satori is the occasion "When Figures show their royal Front." The world appears as a majestic spectacle of magical Becoming.

In the final two lines she speaks of her commitment as a decision already taken;

> Behold the Atom – I preferred –
> To all the lists of Clay!

The meaning of "Atom" is here dictated by the dialectic atom/ clay: it is the essential unit, the sine qua non. Scientifically speaking, we regard the atom as the smallest particle of a chemical element that can exist & still be that particular element. In transcendental terms Buddha Mind is the indivisible phenomenon, the Oneness that makes each of us a human being. Essentially then, Dickinson is here declaring "Verdict for ED!" – meaning that ED has won this round.

It is relevant to cite a similar use of "Atom" in P-376 ("Of Course – I prayed"). In this poem ED is troubled by her civil war, & her inability to commit to the Higher Self, & says,

> 'Twere better Charity
> To leave me in the Atom's Tomb –
> Merry, & Nought, & gay, & numb –
> Than this smart Misery.

Here the ego-self is clearly defined as "Atom's Tomb." The everyday, conventional ego-identity is "Merry, & Nought, & gay, & numb." Ego always buries Buddha six feet under.

870

Finding is the first Act
The second, loss,
Third, Expedition for
The "Golden Fleece"
Fourth, no Discovery –
Fifth, no Crew –
Finally, no Golden Fleece –
Jason – sham – too.

SEEKING THE TREASURE HARD TO FIND

This epigrammatic poem, like many others by ED, poses the question of whether she is generalizing about egocentric life, or about the transcendentalist experience. She describes a life experience as a series of "Acts" involving a changing ego-awareness, which leads me to see the poem as a description of her own fluctuating storyline.

The life she describes is an unfolding drama involving a progressive change in the protagonist, who, by the sixth act has been reduced to a state of miserable skepticism.

The first act applies to us all, as we are born into a given society. We begin life as growing babes, who "find" an ego-identity conditioned by parents & society ("socialization").

Act two is "loss" – which, in transcendentalist experience, is enlightenment, or loss of faith in the reality of the ego-self. Most people do not experience act two; they remain in act one from cradle to grave. For the transcendentalist, however, act two —loss of ego-identity—is the first crucial event in their spiritual evolution.

Act three is the "Expedition for / The 'Golden Fleece'". I recognize the Golden Fleece as belonging to the archetype called the Treasure Hard to Find (one of Jung's favorite themes). The Treasure Hard to Find appears in many different forms, as any reader of the Grimm tales will recall. It is widely known as the pot of gold at the end of the rainbow, the rainbow being the bridge between conscious & unconscious that makes possible spiritual integration of the two realms.

In Buddhist terms, the great prize is an actualized nirvana forever transcending the egocentric world of samsara. Act four leads ED to believe that there is no such thing as an actualized nirvana; act five denies the existence of any "Crew." The Buddhist recognizes that these thoughts are false; but ED was isolated in a New England village, where there was no "crew," no supporting network — what the Buddhists call a sangha, or community. So "finally" the seeker (Jason/ED) is a sham, someone pretending to be what he or she is not. This commonly happens to American Buddhists, unsure of their "success," despairing of their ability to progress. Buddhist teachers attribute this to the fact that Americans are success-oriented, & so misunderstand what their practice is suppose to accomplish.* If American Buddhists can feel this way, even with the support of a "crew," it is not surprising that ED could be overwhelmed at times by the absence of any support, feeling that she might be a sham. Hence I read this poem as the honest expression of discouragement, one of many examples of how ED experienced the Dark Night of the Soul.

---

* This is a regular subject of discussion in the three principal American Buddhist periodicals, Tricycle, Buddhadharma, & Shambhala Sun.

33

If recollecting were forgetting,
Then I remember not.
And if forgetting, recollecting,
How near I had forgot.
And if to miss, were merry,
And to mourn were gay,
How very blithe the fingers
That gathered this, Today!

LEARNING TO REMEMBER

In this early poem ED is not expressing emotion, but rather discussing it. The discussion takes the form of paradox, thanks to the inherent duality of ED/Emily Dickinson. Oversimplifying for the sake of clarity, we might say that Emily Dickinson remembers what ED forgets, & that ED remembers what Emily Dickinson forgets. In her everyday life among family & friends, Emily Dickinson must "forget" (suppress) the Higher Self; in her ego-transcendent episodes ED "transcends ego," just as the term says.

In the present poem ED sums up the situation with her gift for terseness, which we may paraphrase: the intensity of recollecting who I am is no more intense than the intensity of forgetting who I am.

ED was a Sagittarian, but here she speaks like a Libran. As a Libran myself, I have always recognized the archetypal significance of this sign, since it expresses the existential reality of my own life. Libra, the Scales, does not signify "balance," but rather a dual relationship between ego & the unconscious. It is a mutual seesawing back & forth between ego-dominance & ego-transcendent awareness.

The most gifted transcendentalists (such as the mystics) become very much aware of a reciprocity between their highs & lows. An ego-transcendent episode can send them flying high; a threatened loss of recurrence can plunge them into the Dark Night of the Soul. However high you can go — you can go equally low. This is the Libran seesaw.

In this early poem ED is already displaying her interest in the psychology of her feelings, & this poem expresses detachment. She finds herself in a very negative state of mind, & regards it "clinically," like a Buddhist meditator observing his or her own mind in motion, without getting involved, as in vipassana, or "insight" meditation.

The transcendentalists are empiricists, speaking from their own personal experience; hence I understand ED to be speaking about her own case, specifically, & not making vague or general statements. The "Libran Dilemma" will become a life-long preoccupation with ED, because her dual life involves an alternating recollecting & forgetting. When ED experiences Buddha Mind, she suddenly "remembers" "who" she is; when Emily Dickinson immerses herself in her daily life, she suddenly "remembers" "who" she is.

This subject evokes the famous Butterfly dream of Chuang Tzu, a follower of Lao Tzu:

> Chuang Tzu dreamt he was a butterfly &, when he
> awoke, did not know if he was a man who had dreamt
> he was a butterfly or a butterfly who was dreaming
> he was a man.

Recalling that psyche is "butterfly" in Greek, I relate to this classic Libran Dilemma: when I am asleep & dreaming, I am ego experiencing myself as Psyche; when I am awake, I am Psyche experiencing Herself as an ego-identity. ED's oeuvre reflects a lifelong dedication to the Libran Dilemma.

458

Like Eyes that looked on Wastes –
Incredulous of Ought
But Blank – & steady Wilderness –
Diversified by Night –

Just Infinites of Nought –
As far as it could see –
So looked the face I looked upon –
So looked itself – on Me –

I offered it no Help –
Because the Cause was Mine –
The Misery a Compact
As hopeless – as divine –

Neither – would be absolved –
Neither would be a Queen
Without the Other – Therefore –
We perish – tho' We reign -

HIGH NOON

This is a highly crafted poem concerning the dual "relationship" between Dickinson & ED, the ego-self & the Higher Self.* Lines 7-8, the heart of the poem read:

> So looked the face I looked upon –
> So looked itself – on Me –

ED is at pains to express the subtlety of a "relationship" that is not a relationship. In P-642 ("Me from Myself – to banish") she calls Dickinson/ED "mutual Monarch," using the singular, not the plural "mutual Monarchs." One thinks of "Siamese twins" like Chang & Eng, paradoxically two-in-one. Absolute awareness involves an ego-self reduced to the barest minimum, with no power to function proactively, but only to be aware of being aware. In the present poem ED hits on a new way to express this interplay of ego & non-ego by exploiting the verb "to look":

> So looked the face I looked upon –
> So looked itself – on Me –

This supposes that Dickinson is the seeker. This first "looked" means "to look" in the sense of "to have the appearance of," as when we say, "He looked his age." Thus, "ED's Presence appeared as the face I seemed to be seeing."

---

* See <u>Solitary Prowess</u>, "A Dual Life," 44-60.

"Face" is a high-frequency word in ED's discourse, & often appears in the sense of "presence," as in P-463:

> I live with Him – I see His face –
> I go no more away

This is akin to ED's expression "Great Nature's Face" in P-978. So in the present poem Dickinson makes the connection between Buddha Mind & ED Mind: "So looked itself – on Me."

The Buddhists call satori "realization." One who has experienced it is "realized." In the present poem Dickinson experiences a similar form of realization: she realizes that Buddha Mind is none other than herself – or rather, her Self.

The entire poem revolves around this realization. The initial stanza describes the visual experience of Empty Mind:

> Like Eyes that looked on Wastes –
> Incredulous of Ought
> But Blank – & steady Wilderness –
> Diversified by Night –

"Wilderness" is one of ED's terms for "Empty Mind," as in P-1233:

> Had I not seen the Sun
> I could have borne the shade
> But Light a newer Wilderness
> My Wilderness has made –

The everyday wilderness of samsara –egocentric life—gives way to the "newer Wilderness." Initially one may feel "disoriented" in the emptiness of cosmic awareness. One is amazed, but "Incredulous of Ought" – totally accepting of the "Truth's superb surprise"

(P-1129). Still, the awareness is a "steady" blank, whether by day or by night: "Diversified by Night," she says.

To return to lines 7-8:

> So looked the face I looked upon –
> So looked itself – on Me –

I take "So" to mean "That's the way the face/presence looked to me as I looked upon it; & that's the way it looked upon me." Which is to say that Buddha Mind saw ego-self as a "wilderness," just as ego-self saw Buddha Mind as a Wilderness. This is naturally part of the Realization: the ego-self is empty, a Wasteland (to use T.S. Eliot's epithet).

The situation in the present poem is what ED elsewhere calls "Noon," as in P-1056, where "Consciousness – is Noon."* Here she describes what we might call High Noon, an apparent confrontation to the death:

> So looked the face I looked upon –
> So looked itself – on Me –

The third stanza describes what promises to be a long-term impasse:

> I offered it no Help –
> Because the Cause was Mine –
> The Misery a Compact
> As hopeless – as divine –

"Cause" here is "undertaking," or "enterprise" – namely spiritual evolving, or individuating (to use the Jungian term). ED's text here is an acute, lovely paradox:

---

* For "Noon" see also poems 63, 287, 297, 420, 512, & 579.

I offered it no Help –
Because the Cause was Mine –

"I, the ego-self, remained receptive, because this enterprise was that of the Higher Me." The "Misery" is the trauma of accepting the heard truth that the ego-self that "you" have taken for granted all along is a nothing: it doesn't exist. This misery is "hopeless," once the truth sinks in. Ego-loss is a traumatic event; & in the final stanza ED calls High Noon a draw:

Neither – would be absolved –
Neither would be a Queen
Without the Other – Therefore –
We perish – tho' We reign –

Neither the ego-self nor the Higher Self would be set free from the "other": Chang & Eng remain conjoined. Both "reign" alternately in Psyche, & both perish alternately. This is the situation that ED will always live with, for better or for worse.*

---

* It is profitable to read P-340 ("Is Bliss then, such Abyss") in the present context: ED is the foot (the natural Self), & Dickinson is the shoe, the culturally acquired veneer.

684

Best Gains – must have the Losses' Test –
To constitute them – Gains -

CREDITS & DEBITS

This epigram is a reflection of the paradoxical dual life that ED led, the life she shared with Emily Dickinson. Both the ego-transcendent mode & the egocentric mode were necessary to the way she arranged her life. Neither could be "banished," as she says in P-642.

In the context of this everyday, existential dynamic, her epigram takes on a double meaning. She says,

> Best Gains – must have the Losses' Test –
> To constitute them – Gains –

As she experiences the shifting values of egocentrism vs. ego transcendence, it becomes clear that "Gains" & "Losses" are always relative to each other. The "binary" style of her inner life meant that either mode could be regarded as a gain or as a loss. Her epigram expresses a hidden relativity, which we may paraphrase as follows: "Is ED a gain? That depends upon what value you attach to the loss of Emily Dickinson. Is Emily Dickinson a gain? That depends upon what value you attach to the loss of ED."

In this context ED's epigram applies universally. It is not uncommon for people to find themselves torn between the inner self & the public ego-persona. Some will suppress the inner self, some with repress it, & still. Others will work out a compromise, as did ED/Emily Dickinson. ED would not be suppressed, as she says, in P-613:

Still! Could themself have peeped –
And seen my Brain – go round –
They might as wise have lodged a Bird
For Treason – in the Pound –

Adolescence is commonly a time when the identity crisis occurs; it was the foundation for the nineteenth-century Romantic Movement, for the Jazz Age, & for the Generation Gap. It was also the foundation for ED's eventual emergence as a poetic voice finally dominating the daily life of our Woman in White.

424

Removed from accident of Loss *
By Accident of Gain
Befalling not my simple Days –
Myself had just to earn –

Of Riches – as unconscious
As is the Brown Malay
Of Pearls in Eastern Waters,
Marked His – What Holiday

Would stir his slow conception –
Had he the power to dream
That but the Dower's fraction –
Awaited even – Him -

LOSS & GAIN

Ego-transcendence transforms your way of perceiving the world. You lose the accustomed subject-object relationship ("I" in here, vs. the world "out there"), & you awaken to Oneness. ED analyses this in P-1071:

> Perception of an object costs
> Precise the Object's loss –
> Perception in itself a Gain
> Replying to its Price –

In the present poem ED describes this loss/gain dynamic in a less abstract, more concrete way. As in P-1071, she begins by contrasting the loss & gain:

> Removed from Accident of Loss
> By Accident of Gain

Satori is, of course, an "Accident," or unforeseen event, whereby one briefly experiences loss of ego, gaining unconditioned awareness. At the writing of the present poem ED is removed in time from her first transcendent experience, "Befalling not my simple Days," she says. This evokes P-990:

> Not all die early, dying young –
> Maturity of Fate
> Is consummated equally
> In Ages, or a Night –

The transcendent revelation signaled her "Maturity of Fate," &
her readiness to receive it demonstrated that she was no longer
in thrall to her naïveté: now she was willing to follow her Higher
Fate.*

With Accident of Gain ED knew that henceforth it was her
calling to discover the inner wealth:

> Myself had just to earn –
> Of Riches – as unconscious
> As is the Brown Malay

Wealth will become one of ED's favored metaphors, akin to the
Gold sought by the transcendentalist alchemists.

Like any realized transcendentalist, ED readily understood
that spiritual progress consists in uniting ego-awareness with
one's unconscious, instinctual nature. From her own self she
had to earn

> Of Riches – unconscious
> As is the Brown Malay
> Of Pearls in Eastern Waters,

ED intuits the connection between her own "non-Western"
experience & Eastern spirituality. In P-452 she returns to this
specific image of the pearl diver:

> The Malay – took the Pearl-
> Not – I – the Earl –
> I – feared the Sea – too much
> Unsanctified – to touch –

---

* This illustrates the saying of the ancient Romans: <u>Ducunt volentem fata,
nolentem trahunt</u> (Fate leads those who are willing; the unwilling, it drags).

Here, social caste made the pedestrian self an outsider to whom "pearl diving" is taboo, for she is "Unsanctified." In P-7 she recognizes the process as sanctification:

> Pearls are the Diver's farthings
> Extorted from the Sea —
> Pinions — the Seraph's wagon
> Pedestrian once — as we —

ED fancies the primitive person —a Malay pearl diver in the present poem—as unaware of the archetypal meaning of what he does. He does not have, with "his slow conception," the "power to dream." I see this as approximately correct, in the sense that he does not have the sophisticated ego that gives us urban Westerners "the power to dream." Being a transcendentalist by temperament, I recognize that the greater my ego, the greater my need for non-ego.

With the union of ego & non-ego (Jung's hieros-gamos), the immense "Dower," or marriage portion becomes available; & all memorable artists take full advantage. In the present poem, the "Dower's fraction" recalls the "Diver's farthings" of P-7.

III. EGO-TRANSCENDENCE
AS ALIENATION

THE TOWN JUGGLER

1170

Nature affects to be sedate
Upon occasion, grand
But let our observation shut
Her practices extend

To Necromancy & the Trades
Remote to understand
Behold our spacious Citizen
Unto a Juggler turned –

What respite from her thrilling toil
Did Beauty ever take –
But Work might be electric Rest
To those that Magic make –
(From P-1585)

THE METAMORPHOSIS

ED recognized that she was a "magician," a "juggler" (cf. F. jongleur, ME jouglere, "minstrel, magician"), for this was her calling. Writing poetry was neither work nor play; it was her "electric rest."

In P-1170, "Nature affects to be sedate," ED contrasts our egocentric observation of Nature with Nature's secret, or occult activities going on behind our backs, when our observation is "shut."

Such is the secret activity of ED, creating a private oeuvre & hiding it away, booklet by booklet, her "slow Riches" of P-843. To her friends & neighbors Dickinson was their "spacious citizen"; but privately, when she retired to her room to make poetry, she was "Unto a Juggler turned."

P-1158 describes the familiar dynamic between magician & audience:

Best Witchcraft is Geometry
To the magician's mind –
His ordinary acts are feats
To thinking of mankind.

His amazing tricks are the result of an intimate science (knowledge) – what ED calls "geometry," alluding to the stage magician's mastery of the space around him.

This is what the poem says, read at face value; but it implies a good deal more. ED realizes that her own brand of magic, intimately familiar to herself —her private science—will appear cryptic & mysterious to her readers, including the "puzzled scholars" of P-501, "This World is not Conclusion."

When the young Emily Dickinson became enlightened, she understood her awakening to be the Great Adventure of human consciousness, for she had been liberated from contingency. She suddenly saw that the relative truth of her life in Amherst was irrelevant to her identity. She was living in a collective illusion where everyone was obediently playing the roles assigned them — & a non-ego reality had suddenly been made accessible to her. This made her an alien — an "illegal alien" as it were, for she had glimpsed a reality transcending the spiritual doctrine of the local elcers. In a trace she had become an apostate, a heretic, in spite of herself, & there was no turning back. The exhilaration & the excitement of her discovery demanded documentation, & she felt herself empowered to create a relevant discourse. If she was now an alien, so be it: this would be her documentation, the authentication of her origin.

If her social self, Emily Dickinson, was to remain respectable, then her apostasy had to be kept secret. When she sat down to write poetry she became a conjuror revealing a magic reality, as she describes it in the present poem:

> To Necromancy & the Trades
> Remote to understand
> Behold our spacious Citizen
> Unto a Juggler turned —

Henceforth she would live a dual life, & create her transcendent discourse in private. She would turn this into booklets crafted for the purpose, & these would become her private stash of P-843:

> I made slow Riches but my Gain
> Was steady as the Sun
> And every Night, it numbered more
> Than the preceding One

This manner of life made her acutely aware of social prejudices regarding "insiders" & "outsiders." She recognized herself as a witch, a natural woman who had no use for patriarchal values. We moderns, living in the twenty-first century, will quickly see the analogy with closeted gays & lesbians, who create a social persona as a strategy for getting on in life.

DOCUMENTED ALIENS

In a number of reflective poems of great immediacy ED documents how certain entities in the natural world are regarded as "misfits" alien to the social order. Here she sees her own condition reflected, after a fashion — in a housefly, a spider, even a mushroom. These poems are among her most poignantly inspired, & probe the anti-nature bias of the patriarchal ontology beginning to yield dire consequences for the Earth Mother.

1746

The most important population
Unnoticed dwell,
They have a heaven each instant
Not any hell.

Their names, unless you know them,
'Twere useless tell.
Of bumble-bees & other nations
The grass is full.

.

AS ABOVE, SO BELOW; AS WITHOUT, SO WITHIN: UNNOTICED ALIENS

ED's temperament is eco-conscious & biocentric by nature; &, like many a modern ecologist, she takes the long-term view concerning the infinite variety of ecosystems with their complex communities, or "populations": they are more important to Gaia than the single community of humankind:

> The most important population
> Unnoticed dwell,
> They have a heaven each instant
> Not any hell.

Psyche is Mother Nature in human form, so the principle follows: as without, so within. Psyche Herself is an ecosystem of instinctual forces, a "Continent," as ED says in P-1354:

> The Heart is the Capital of the Mind –
> The Mind is a single State –
> The Heart & the Mind together make
> A single Continent –
>
> One – is the Population –
> Numerous enough –
> This ecstatic Nation
> Seek – it is Yourself.

Within the economy of Psyche it is true that "The most important population / Unnoticed dwell," these being the contents of the creative unconscious: ED says "Unnoticed," where we say "repressed." The alchemists said, "As above, so below" (quod superis, sicut quod inferius), where "above" means "conscious," & "below" means "unconscious." This is known as the Hermetic Doctrine of Correspondences: the world reality of our conscious mind, "out there," corresponds to the world reality of our unconscious mind, the "ecstatic Nation," as ED calls it.

In P-1746 ED says of the unnoticed population,

> They have a heaven each instant
> Not any hell.

This is the "ecstatic Nation" that she, as witness/poet is continually "noticing," & seeking within.

Pairing these two poems as we have done makes it tolerably clear that both take the creative unconscious as their subject:

> Their names, unless you know them,
> "Twere useless tell.
> Of bumble-bees & other nations
> The grass is full.

ED devotes her expressive powers to "telling" of these inner forces. So far, it appears to be "useless" to do so, if we are to judge by what her commentators have to say. She supplies many names & descriptions (her unique "coinages," as I call them*), but these have so far passed quite "Unnoticed."

---

*   Some examples of these internal goings-on identified by ED: "Eternal Function," the "Profound Experiment," "Maturity of Fate," the "Double Estate," "Death's Sing Privacy," the "Crash Without a Sound," the "Crash of Nothing," "Anonymous Delight," "Phantom Queen," "Electric Rest," etc., etc. These coinages (& many more) will be duly accounted for in a Glossary.

The last two lines of P-1746 implicitly contrast "outer" Nature with the "inner" biome:

> Of bumble-bees & other nations
> The grass is full.

Such nations in the grass do not "dwell unnoticed"; on the contrary, they have been freely observed & described countless times; but "The most important population" is the one within:

> This ecstatic Nation
> Seek – it is Yourself.

DOCUMENTED ALIENS

The Bat (P-1575)

The Housefly (P-1388)

The Bee (P-1035, P-1405, P-916)

The Rat (P-1356), & The Rattrap (P-1340)

The Butterfly (P-129, P-1658)

The Spider (P-1167, P-605)

The Mushroom (P-1298)

The Bobolink (P-755)

The Drunkard (P-1645)

1575

The Bat is dun, with wrinkled Wings —
Like fallow Article —
And not a song pervade his Lips —
Or none perceptible.

His small Umbrella quaintly halved
Describing in the Air
An Arc alike inscrutable
Elate Philosopher.

Deputed from what Firmament —
Of what Astute Abode —
Empowered with what Malignity
Auspiciously withheld —

To his adroit Creator
Ascribe no less the praise —
Beneficent, believe me,
His Eccentricities -

Skepticism, especially since the Enlightenment, has come to mean disbelief —primarily religious disbelief—& the skeptic has often been likened to the village atheist.*

BATWOMAN

ED begins this description of the bat by noting its drabness & apparent shortcomings: it is like a "fallow Article." I take "Article" in the sense of "thing": the bat seems to be an imperfect being, uncultivated, or left fallow by evolution, as it were. It is a mammal that took to the air, like the birds, but it has no song, "Or none perceptible," at least. (It does make a shrill, mouselike noise, but this can't be perceived as a "song").

ED compares the unpredictable flight of the bat to the unpredictable thinking of the "inscrutable / Elate philosopher." By "Elate" is most likely meant "Eleactic."** If ED identified with any school of philosophy, it would certainly be the Skeptics. The Eleactic*** philosophers —notably Parmenides & Zeno—questions (like ED) any knowledge beyond the contents of one's own personal, empirical experience.

If any critter is symbolic of the Skeptic, it is the bat, the "renegade mammal" traditionally identified by the mainstream with the Powers of Darkness. The Skeptic (Gk. Skeptikos, "inquirer") is one who is unsatisfied with the received dogmas, & is regarded as a heretic, anathema to the ruling class, & fair game for persecution. The skeptics have always seemed "inscrutable"

---

* The New Encyclopaedia Britannica, 15ᵗʰ ed., "Skepticism" (vol. 25, 590).

** Misspellings do occur in the Canon, whether by miscopying, or by misreading (cf. P-304, Jew/Jewel, & P-457, Pearl/Purl). One must be extremely chary, however, of such judgment calls.

*** From Elea, an ancient town in Southern Italy.

to the mainstream, just as ED's critics commonly regard her poetry as "cryptic," or "enigmatic." They are inside the box; the skeptics are outside.

As a "renegade mammal"* the bat is traditionally regarded as a creature of the dark, & so is "malign," a form taken by the Devil. It is not difficult to see how ED might relate to the bat as a renegade, a deserter from the faith. In P-1617 ("To try to speak, & miss the way") she alludes to herself as "the Mutineer / Whose title is 'the Soul'." She was engaged in a heretical activity. As poet, she flew by night; &, as the years went on (this is a late poem), she was considered to be batty.

The third stanza sums up ED's self-image in terms of how she would be regarded by the community, were her clandestine activity to become known:

> Deputed from what Firmament –
> Of what Astute Abode –
> Empowered with what Malignity
> Auspiciously withheld –

ED similarly regarded the unpredictable flight of the butterfly, considered suspect by the straitlaced community. In P-1685 she writes:

> Because he travels freely
> And wears a proper coat
> The circumspect are certain
> That he is dissolute –

She herself, as she made her booklets & stashed them away, was "withholding auspiciously" what would surely be regarded as the

---

* I owe this term to H. G. Baynes' lucid discussion of the symbolism of the bat (Mythology of the Soul, 776-7).

"malignity" of her non-Christian experience of reality. She would be regarded as a witch, with a bat as her familiar.

"Auspiciously withheld" defines ED's approach to the problem presented by the writing of her poetry: should she publish it, or should she keep it secret? She took the auspices −& withheld it. What she had to say as an oracular poet was bound to be misunderstood.

In the final stanza, however, ED expresses the inner satisfaction she derives from her inscrutable "Eccentricities":

> To his adroit Creator
> Ascribe no less the praise −
> Beneficent, believe me,
> His Eccentricities −

She knows that her subliminal existence in the Twilight Zone is "Beneficent" − "believe me!" she says − & only she can be the judge of that.

1388

Those Cattle smaller than a Bee
That herd upon the eye –
Whose tillage is the passing Crumb –
Those Cattle are the Fly –
Of Barns for Winter – blameless –
Extemporaneous stalls
They found to our objection –
On eligible walls –
Reserving the presumption
To suddenly descend
And gallop on the Furniture –
Or odiouser offend –
Of their peculiar calling
Unqualified to judge
To Nature we remand them
To justify or scourge -

A PECULIAR CALLING

As a student of Latin, ED knows that the common housefly is called <u>musca domestica</u>, literally, "domestic intruder." What it has in common with cattle is that it is a "domestic" creature; "domestic" means not only "domesticated," but also "frequenting human habitations."

She finds the fly's intrusion to be "blameless" (line 5), just as in P-1167 (one of the spider poems) she sees no offense:

> But what redress can be
> For an offense nor here nor there
> So not in Equity —

That is to say, Nature does not intrude upon man; man intrudes upon Nature.

The present poem was probably occasioned by the hot weather, when flies are most active (they "gallop on the Furniture / Or odiouser offend"*). ED is not judgmental here: she recognizes only that the housefly has a "peculiar calling," which of course she knew to be true of herself — a peculiar calling determined by Nature. In this matter egocentric people are "Unqualified to judge" (line 14). Ultimately Nature is the judge:

---

* ED's readers will recognize "odiouser" as characteristic of her style, which affords many eamples of the bold comparative calling attention to itself: "supremer" (P-232), "possibler" (P-351), "infiniter" (P-625), "durabler" (P-1192), etc. (Cf. our common usage, "more unique," which ED would express as "uniquer," no doubt.)

> To Nature we remand them
> To justify or scourge –

"To remand" means "to return to custody, pending trial." It is of some interest that ED uses this expression here, in reference to flies as cattle; for in P-1524 ("A faded Boy – in sallow Clothes") she says that the cattle tended by the boy are "Remanded to a Ballad's Barn." She means that the old traditional rural ways are gradually disappearing, & that they are given into the custody of poets & painters (like Grandma Moses). In the present poem, the judgment handed down must be left up to Nature.

I believe that a case can be made for ED's identification here with the fly, considering the well-known & ancient metaphor of the gadfly as a critical person who irritates the status quo, like the poets barred from Plato's Republic.

Emily Dickinson was always aware of her status as an outsider: ED was the "intruder," the <u>musca domestica</u>, whose overt presence would be an affront to a peaceful, Christian, New England village. Like Siamese twins, Emily Dickinson & ED shared the same Psyche: this was their "peculiar calling." ED is Psyche, Mother Nature in human form, & Emily Dickinson recognizes her as the Fountain wherein she drinks. The poems attributed to Emily Dickinson must be remanded to Nature, "To justify or scourge."

1035

Bee! I'm expecting you!
Was saying Yesterday
To Somebody you know
That you were due –

The Frogs got Home last Week –
Are settled, & at work –
Birds, mostly back –
The Clover warm & thick –

You'll get my Letter by
The seventeenth; Reply
Or better, be with me -
Yours, Fly.

TRANSCENDENT ECOLOGY: THE FLY SPEAKS

Satori is the consciousness of Oneness, of reality as completely interconnected, like Indra's Net. Most importantly, one's own Self is the center of this Net. One belongs in the dharma, for it is our original home, our residence, our abode. Satori is a soaring homecoming, a flight like that of the balloon in P-1630:

> Ascension that for which it was,
> Its soaring Residence.

To awaken as one with Nature is to be, as ED says in P-304,

> A Guest in this stupendous place –
> The Parlor – of the Day –

She is the grateful guest who makes herself "at home."

In the present poem ED describes a fantasy or reverie, where she is one with the other creatures of Nature. Normally the ego-self lives separated from the world "out there," but ego-transcendence returns one to the heart of things, where you experience yourself as one more element in the ecosystem. The other critters are your close neighbors, your "kinsmen" (to use one of ED's terms*).

In the present poem a housefly is writing a friendly letter to the bee, & begins by mentioning ED, their mutual friend:

---

* See poems 380, 645, 885, 1137, 1709.

Bee! I'm expecting you!
Was saying Yesterday
To Somebody you know
That you were due –

With the passing mention of ED – a throwaway line – the fly includes her in the shared ecosystem as one of their own. Here she is not like the other human beings, the ones who swat flies & exploit bees. Truth be told, <u>those</u> are the original aliens, the conquistadors come to despoil the land.

The fly goes on to relate the relevant news as a farmer might do, & ends by urging its kinsman to reply:

You'll get my Letter by
The seventeenth; Reply
Or better, be with me –
Yours, Fly.

This complimentary close is actually the punch line. The beginning of the poem does not prepare you for an epistolary poem. It isn't a salutation, ("Dear Bee"), but rather an apostrophe, & you naturally assume that ED herself is speaking, as elsewhere, apostrophizing Nature. In P-722, for example, she says, "Sweet Mountains – Ye tell Me no lie." P-1320 is presented as a letter to the month of March: "Dear March – Come in."

Housefly, the home intruder, is with us year-round, a continual resident, like ED herself, & so shares a close acquaintance with the family, unlike that of the seasonal visitor.

The last line, "Yours, Fly," is of peculiar interest, because of its haiku-like simplicity. "Fly" is a very general, monosyllabic vocable referring to freedom, & ED, in Amherst, was the fly in Dickinson's ointment, the domestic intruder whose nature was to fly, to soar – & of course to avoid being swatted. That's why she hid her poems.

1405

Bees are Black, with Gilt Surcingles –
Buccaneers of Buzz.
Ride abroad in ostentation
And subsist on Fuzz.

Fuzz ordained – not Fuzz contingent –
Marrows of the Hill.
Jugs – a Universe's fracture
Could not jar or spill

916

His Feet are shod with Gauze –
His Helmet, is of gold,
His Breast, a Single Onyx
With Chrysophrase, inlaid.

His Labor is a Chant –
His Idleness – a Tune –
Oh, for a Bee's experience
Of Clovers, & of Noon!

THE BALLAD OF THE BEE

The Honeybee is not an "alien" like the housefly, its kinsman who sends it a friendly letter: "Bee! I'm expecting you!" (P-1035). Its natural ways, however —its self-contained society—is its own reason for being in the non-human world, away from our society. Human beings have simply conquered an alien society so as to exploit it selfishly, as a honey factory. Needless to say, ED relates to the bee as an agent beyond the aims & intentions of beekeepers, just as Buddha Mind exists beyond the aims & intentions of city hall.

The two poems presented here are sportive & carefree, celebrating the bee as if in ballad. In P-1405 she announces that the bee is black, with golden bands (as people may think that the zebra is black, with white stripes). Since the surcingle is a bellyband for a horse (to keep the saddle in place), it suggests that the bee wears ornamental bands that contrast with its black "coat."

ED's readers are well aware of how she admired the bee. It is a yang force of Nature, proactive, like herself, & so she identifies, as in P-230, "We — Bee & I — live by quaffing." The bee appears as a kind of lama, with a lifelong devotion to the Spirit:

> His Labor is a Chant —
> His Idleness — a Tune —

Further, the bee grazes on blossoms as it were; it subsists "on Fuzz, / Fuzz ordained — not Fuzz contingent." To "subsist on Fuzz" is to live plainly, not indulgently. "Fuzz" figures large in P-1405, as if it, not the bee, were the real subject of the discourse:

> And subsist on Fuzz.
> Fuzz ordained – not Fuzz contingent –

"Ordained" has two meanings: 1) "established by authority, & 2) "foreordained, destined." The latter, non-ego meaning, occurs in P-34:

> Nature in charity –
> Nature in equity –
> The Rose ordained!

The bee feeds on its natural nourishment, not on "contingent" food, as do people, whose diet varies according to circumstances – which is to say that ego's ways of nourishing itself are always contingent. The Higher Self, ED, discovers that her nourishment is foreordained. It is the natural nourishment of all human beings, "preconcerted with itself," (P-290), "Predestined to unfold" (P-1697).

The bee visits the chalices of blossoms,

> Jugs – a Universe's fracture
> Could not jar or spill.

Which is to say, satori, the Great Shatterer, spills not a drop of the intoxicating soma. With the "Universe's fracture" one turns on, tunes in, & drops out, without waiting for Dr. Hofmann to synthesize lysergic acid.

1356

The Rat is the concisest Tenant.
He pays no Rent.
Repudiates the Obligation –
On Schemes intent

Balking our Wit
To sound or circumvent –
Hate cannot harm
A Foe so reticent –
Neither Decree prohibit him –
Lawful as Equilibrium.

> The rat is no less marvelous than the elephant as a
> finder & maker of the way. It has a peculiar talent
> for entering buildings... & is wonderfully successful
> in overcoming whatever defenses men can put in its
> path.
>
> – H. Zimmer, <u>The Art of Indian Asia</u>, 46.

THE INTRUDER

P-1340, "A Rat surrendered here," written at about the same time as the present poem, is actually about the rattrap as a symbol of samsara, the illusory dual, ego-reality that kills, or represses, the original non-ego mind with which we are born. P-1356, the present poem, centers on the rat itself as one of the alien entities intruding on our domestic order & tranquility. I say "intruding" advisedly, recalling that the housefly is named <u>musca domestica</u> in Latin, meaning "domestic intruder."

Of the rat, a major domestic intruder, ED says,

> The Rat is concisest Tenant.
> He pays no Rent.
> Repudiates the Obligation –
> On Schemes intent

The rat is more like a squatter than a tenant, but ED does not really regard the rat as "illegal." Her irony is palpable: the rat's lease is so concise that its terms are non-existent! The rat is a schemer, as Zimmer notes in our epigraph: he "is wonderfully successful in overcoming whatever defenses men can put in its path."

We are all disgusted by the rat, & even terrified of it; but ED's poem (like Zimmer's observation) involves no emotional attitude:

> Balking our Wit
> To sound or circumvent –
> Hate cannot harm
> A Foe so reticent –
> Neither Decree prohibit him –
> Lawful as Equilibrium.

I take "sound" in the sense of "fathom." Man, however elaborate his civilizations, is impotent to outwit the rat in the competition for survival. In fact, the rat, as the carrier of a certain flea, spread the bubonic plague in fourteenth-century Europe, killing millions. ED has a different point to make.

She possessed a natural understanding of what we now call ecology, literally "study of habitat." No creature can be "outlawed," because, in the balance, or equilibrium, of nature, everything exists "lawfully," i.e., according to natural law. "Natural law" is another name for the dharma, the way everything is, regardless of how ego sees it. We say, "If a tree falls in the forest, & non one is there, does it make a noise?" This is like asking whether the dharma exists in the absence of ego. The present poem is about how the rat is, in the absence of ego.

ED's dry objectivity here comes from the recognitions that satori reveals the presence of Buddha Mind, & that Buddha Mind is the subject of the poem. It is no coincidence that Zimmer recognizes the rat as "wonderfully successful in overcoming whatever defenses men can put in its path." Buddha Mind has always been viewed with hatred & fear by the Christian patriarchy, obsessed with the notion of heresy, as attested by the Spanish Inquisition. ED was fully aware that her life in the dharma

made her an outlaw. It also made her "the concisest poet," &
a "reticent foe' of the System. She herself embodied the truth
that ego-transcendence cannot be banned by law; neither can it
be harmed by hate, ostracism, or proscription. She makes note
of this in P-538:

> "Tis true – They shut me in the Cold –
> But then – Themselves were warm
> And could not know the feeling 'twas –
> Forget it – Lord – of Them –

She goes on to recognize that "The Harm They did – was
short." Turns out that for a favored few, repression of Buddha
Mind is not tantamount to death, after all. Egocentricism,
though it monopolize the planet, cannot "sound or circumvent"
Enlightenment in every single instance.

1340

A Rat surrendered here
A brief career of Cheer
And Fraud & Fear.

Of Ignominy's due
Let all addicted to
Beware.

The most obliging Trap
Its tendency to snap
Cannot resist —

Temptation is the Friend
Repugnantly resigned
At last.

Earth at the best
Is but a scanty Toy –
Bought, carried Home
To Immortality.

It looks so small
We chiefly wonder then
At our Conceit
In purchasing.

(From P-1024)

CAVEAT EMPTOR

This poem by ED is reminiscent of Robert Burns, whose poetry
finds other echoes in her work.* She writes here of a rat whose
plans went awry:

A Rat surrendered here
A brief career of Cheer
And Fraud & Fear.

This observation articulates a dharma truth which comes to light
suddenly & dramatically when satori strikes; the ego-self lives "A
brief career of Cheer / And Fraud & Fear." It seeks happiness,
deludes itself, & dreads death. The egocentric, contingent reality
of samsara is a trap that spares no one:

Of Ignominy's due
Let all addicted to
Beware.

---

* See P-492 & P-1314, & notice her borrowings.

It is a humiliating defeat in the end. ED calls it "Ignominy," because the word is rooted in ignorare. Egocentric life is a life of ignorance, & we all become deeply addicted to it.

> The most obliging Trap
> Its tendency to snap
> Cannot resist –

Samsara is "The most obliging Trap." It smothers us in its embrace, for that is its nature.

> Temptation is the Friend
> Repugnantly resigned
> At last.

Ego, in its incessant search for gratification, takes temptation as its guides. Temptation, in fact, defines ego to a large extent, & we all, at last, renounce it "Repugnantly." ED is most likely using this word with the literal meaning of the L. re-pugnare, "to fight against." We go off kicking & screaming.

The rattrap as an analogy of samsara conveys the idea that samsara, as relative truth, virtually always kills Buddha Mind for good. The fortunate few who find their way free can look back & post a warning to the rest of us: Beware! Many a sutra amounts to just such a warning.

129

Cocoon above! Cocoon below!
Stealthy Cocoon, why hide you so
What all the world suspect?
An hour, & gay on every tree
Your secret, perched in ecstasy
Defies imprisonment!

An hour in Chrysalis to pass,
Then gay above receding grass
A Butterfly to go!
A moment to interrogate,
Then wiser than a "Surrogate,"
The Universe to know!

ALIENATION MAKES THE ALIEN

In this early poem Dickinson, as a young woman, gives voice to her recognition that she is not to live with the freedom that men take for granted. Observing a number of cocoons she has discovered, she experiences them as <u>natural freedom</u>: freedom is the unhampered Becoming of instinct, & it is the same for one & all. Dickinson was early aware that her gender worked against her instinctual need to be free; the locus classicus is P-77, which begins,

> I never hear the word "escape"
> Without a quicker blood,
> A sudden expectation,
> A flying attitude!

In the present poem ED's description of the cocoon is inspired by her own experience as secret poet. Ideally her poetry would 1) slowly germinate in the dark, until it was ready to emerge, & 2) be published, joyfully "perched in ecstasy" on the printed page as it were, where it would "defy imprisonment!" That is the proper way for a poet to live, free & uncensored, both in her works & in her person. Had Dickinson known the social freedom of action accorded to all men, she would have "The Universe to know!" She would fly high, "interrogate" the world by confronting it directly, & know what cannot be known by reading books, the "surrogates" for reality.

Of course ED's experience of satori taught her a higher

freedom — the highest, as a matter of fact: freedom not only from the tyranny of the patriarchal ego, but more importantly, freedom from the tyranny of her own ego as an internalized form of that same external authority. I believe that her deep sense of alienation was what led to ego-transcendence. She, like the Butterfly of P-1099, had "The Aptitude to fly."

1685

The butterfly obtains
But little sympathy
Though favorably mentioned
In Entomology –

Because he travels freely
And wears a proper coat
The circumspect are certain
That he is dissolute –

Had he the homely scutcheon
Of modest Industry
'Twere fitter certifying
For Immortality -

THE SOLITARY DRINKER

Public opinion is generally mistaken as to anyone's private character or worth. This fact was paramount in the life of ED, since she led two lives, one public, one secret. Outwardly she was a New England homemaker; inwardly she was a Monarch Butterfly.

The flamboyant appearance of the butterfly does not reflect the staid mind-set of a nineteenth-century New England village. In P-80 ED expresses a similar idea in terms of Switzerland & Italy:

> Our lives are Swiss —
> So still — so Cool —
> Till some odd afternoon
> The Alps neglect their Curtains
> And we look farther on!
>
> *Italy* stands the other side!
> While like a guard between —
> The solemn Alps —
> The siren Alps
> Forever intervene!

Like Italy, the Butterfly evokes a brilliant Renaissance; ED, the Monarch Butterfly, guarded her secret enterprise. "Who am I," she says in P-173,

> To tell the pretty secret
> Of the Butterfly!

ED supposes that the striking beauty of the freely flying butterfly is lost on the sober citizens of Amherst, "often seen — but seldom felt, / On our New England Farms," as she says in P-1407. In the privacy of her poetry she "travels freely / And wears a proper coat"; but the locals are ants who disapprove of grasshoppers & butterflies.

If the butterfly presented a plain appearance, looking like Emily Dickinson (say), with a "homely scucheon" ("meek escutcheon' in P-98), then it would be easier to qualify for Heaven (the churchgoer's idea of "Immortality"), as a God-fearing member of society. ED knew that there was no God to fear.

Thus the present poem is actually an explanation of why ED recognized secrecy as necessary to her poetic enterprise. Privately, she was "dissolute," & recognized ego-transcendence as an addictive intoxication, as in P-214, "I taste a liquor never brewed," where she describes herself, unforgettably, as "the little Tippler / Leaning against the — Sun."

1167

Alone & in a Circumstance
Reluctant to be told
A spider on my reticence
Assiduously crawled

And so much more at Home than I
Immediately grew
I felt myself a visitor
And hurriedly withdrew

Revisiting my late abode
With articles of claim
I found it quietly assumed
As a Gymnasium
Where Tax asleep & Title off
The inmates of the Air
Perpetual presumption took
As each were special Heir –
If any strike me on the street
I can return the Blow –
If any take my property
According to the Law
The Statute is my Learned friend
But what redress can be
For an offense nor here nor there
So not in Equity –
That Larceny of time & mind
The marrow of the Day
By spider, or forbid it Lord
That I should specify.

> The fairest Home I ever knew
> Was founded in an Hour
> By Parties also that I knew
> A spider & a Flower –
> A manse of mechlin & of Floss –
>
> (P-1423)

SPIDERWOMAN

ED related strongly to the spider, as evidenced by her several poems (e.g., 605, 1138, 1275, 1423, & the present poem). The Jungian symbolist H. G. Baynes has commented at length on the archetype of the spider as a mediator between the creative instinct & the ego-consciousness,* strongly suggested by P-1138:

> A Spider sewed at Night
> Without a Light
> Upon an Arc of White.
>
> If Ruff it was of Dame
> Or Shroud of Gnome
> Himself himself inform.
>
> Of Immortality
> His Strategy
> Was Physiognomy.

Here the spider works in the dark, as a force of the creative unconscious, making a web that could be identified with either

---

* <u>Mythology of the Soul</u>, 754 et sqq.

realm — that of the gnome underground, or that of the fashionable lady.*

In P-1275, "The Spider as an Artist," ED recognizes that she & the spider are of a kind, & writes:

> Neglected Son of Genius
> I take thee by the Hand —

The present poem is one of ED's "long" poems, a meditation on an incident that occurred between her & a spider. In relating the anecdote, she begins with a disclaimer:

> Alone & in a Circumstance
> Reluctant to be told
> A spider on my reticence
> Assiduously crawled

This evokes Cervantes' famous opening sentence: "In a village of La Mancha, whose name is neither here nor there…" ED found herself alone & in a circumstance not pertinent to the case.

She says that the spider "Assiduously crawled" on her "reticence." This is akin to P-1448:

> How soft a Caterpillar steps —
> I find one on my Hand
> From such a velvet world it comes
> Such plushes at command

---

* "Physiognomy" may well be a pun on "Gnome," i.e., the web is the outer appearance of the Gnome, a winding-sheet. In a letter to Higginson ED signs off as "Your Gnome"; the editor, Thomas Johnson, suggests that "perhaps he had earlier commented on the gnomic quality of her verses" (Emily Dickinson: Selected Letters, 182-3.)

Women who are culturally programmed react hysterically to the sudden appearance of a mouse or spider ("Eek!"); not so ED. She remains observant, silent, "reticent." As in the caterpillar poem, ED immediately senses that Emily Dickinson is the alien here, not the spider. She, not the spider, has trespassed (lines 5-8). When Emily Dickinson transcends, she becomes ED Spiderwoman, the one writing this poem about Emily Dickinson the intruder. Just as in Navajo & Hopi legends, ED Spiderwoman is the mediator between the instinctual unconscious & the ego-consciousness that turns underground activity into a recognizable Physiognomy.

Beginning with line 9, ED tells how she revisited the spot —her "late abode"—& recognizes it now as a "Gymnasium." "Gymnasium," in the European sense (the one meant here) is a prep school; but ED was certainly aware that "gymnasium" originally meant exercising naked (Gk. Gymnos, "naked"). Ego-transcendence is "naked consciousness," consciousness divested of the local ego-costume, the "Costumeless Consciousness" of P-1454. Naked consciousness, consciousness sans ego, is a "Gymnasium of a Higher Order," where one exercises the powers of the creative unconscious.

Here, the notion of property (Tax, title) does not exist. Here is the free realm of the "Air," as described in P-1060:

> Air has no Residence, no Neighbor,
> No Ear, no Door,
> No Apprehension of Another
> Oh, Happy Air!

Nature is Earth & Air, where every "inmate" lives a "gay apostasy," as in P-1526:

> His oriental heresies
> Exhilarate the Bee,
> And filling all the Earth & Air
> With gay apostasy

Of course ED is the one experiencing the "apostasy," a sense of liberation, abandoning Emily Dickinson's constant loyalty to an egocentric, law-abiding community.

One of the charms of ED's satirical style is her fondness for pseudolegalese, as in lines 14-16:

> The inmates of the Air
> Perpetual presumption took
> As each were special Heir –

"Presumption" is a legal term meaning "inference from known facts." Each of Nature's critters, living freely, according to instinct, "infers" from its habitat that it is a "special Heir of the Air," an "Air Heir."

In lines 17-21 she notes how daily behavior is regulated by our laws:

> If any strike me on the street
> I can return the Blow –
> If any take my property
> According to the Law
> The Statute is my Learned friend

"My Learned friend: is a polite cliché in legalese, referring to another lawyer; at the same time it means "acquired, not innate." Egocentric life in all its ramifications, is our "Learned friend."*

---

* "Learned" with two syllables, of course, as in the name of the noted American jurist, Judge Learned Hand (1872-1961).

Beginning with line 22 ED puts to us a rhetorical question, as if we, her readers, were members of the jury in this Trial of the Spider, & she its defense attorney:

> But what redress can be
> For an offense nor here nor there
> So not in Equity –

I can hear her adding, "ladies & gentlemen of the jury?" She maintains that the "offense" is non-existent, neither here nor there (line 23) – "So not in Equity."

"Equity," in legalese, means "the application of general principles of justice to correct or supplement the law" (Oxford English Dictionary); therefore, she argues, the rules of Equity is irrelevant to the action of the accused Spider. Legal restraints do not apply here in the first place, so there is no redress called for.

Line 25 names the basic issues in this courtroom trial: "That Larceny of time & mind." "Larceny" means "theft" – specifically, "the unlawful taking of personal property with intent to deprive the rightful owner of it permanently" (Merriam-Webster). Here ED sums up ego-transcendence, albeit satirically. Society at large considers ego-transcendence to be a theft of time (clock time) & mind (ego-self). For society, clock time & ego make up "The marrow of the day," the essential part of daily life. ED's encounter with the Spider triggered satori; but Spider is not the culprit. The culprit is – who? "Forbid it, Lord, that I should specify."

605

The Spider holds a Silver Ball
In unperceived Hands –
And dancing softly to Himself
His Yarn of Pearl – unwinds –

He plies from Nought to Nought –
In unsubstantial Trade –
Supplants our Tapestries with His –
In half the period –

An Hour to rear supreme
His Continents of Light –
Then dangle from the Housewife's Broom –
His Boundaries – forgot –

> He lay looking at the ceiling, which was dark with
> smoke; cobwebs dangled from the tiles like tapestry.
> "She ought to clean it & not expect me to have to
> see such things," he said to himself angrily.*

The spider in this poem is one of ED's most remarkable documented aliens, because it is a self-portrait rendered in vivid detail. ED understands only too clearly the analogy between herself & the arachnid:

> The Spider holds a Siver Ball
> In unperceived Hands –
> And dancing softly to Himself
> His Yarn of Pearl – unwinds –

ED spins from a sphere within, held "In unperceived Hands," & dances softly to herself as she unwinds her "Yarn of Pearl." The "Yarn" she spins is the ongoing narrative of her wild adventure on the sea of human becoming.

In the second stanza she defines the nature of her enterprise:

> He plies from Nought to Nought –
> In unsubstantial Trade –
> Supplants our Tapestries with His –
> In half the period –

The spider does not build upon any preexisting infrastructure, nor does ED create her work within any preexisting tradition. She comes out of nowhere, & has no goal: she is sui generis. She has nothing to do with the tapestry of American letters, &, in short order, supplants "American" poetry with an archetypal weaving alien to any American tradition.

---

*   R.K. Narayan, <u>The Financial Expert</u>, 41.

ED recognized that each human being is as a "Continent":

> An Hour to rear supreme
> His Continents of Light –
> Then dangle from the Housewife's Broom –
> His Boundaries – forgot –

In P-1354 she notes,

> The Heart & the Mind together make
> A single Continent –

Any given poem/sutra by her is a Continent –a Container, if you will—as she ays to Hernando de Soto, in P-832:

> Soto! Explore thyself!
> Therein thyself shalt find
> The "Undiscovered Continent" –
> No Settler had the Mind.

As householder, ED was ever aware of the boundaries between herself & Dickinson. Her familiars were all involved mainly in the daily life of family & friends; who among them would be able to regard her creations as "Continents of Light"? Which is to say, who would be able to recognize Enlightenment as the unconditioned reality? To date this has not even occurred to any of ED's commentators.

1298

The Mushroom is the Elf of Plants –
At Evening, it is not –
At morning, in a Truffled Hut
It stop upon a Spot

As if it tarried always
And yet its whole Career
Is shorter than a Snake's Delay
And fleeter than a Tare –

'Tis Vegetation's Juggler –
The Germ of alibi –
Doth like a Bubble antedate
And like a Bubble, hie –

I feel as if the Grass was pleased
To have it intermit –
This surreptitious scion
Of Summer's circumspect.

Had Nature any supple Face
Or could she one contemn –
Had Nature an Apostate –
That Mushroom – it is Him!

AN APOSTATE IN THE YARD

The toadstool appears here as a kind of magical growth. Robert Graves has noted that "throughout the world mushrooms were believed to be begotten by lightning."* Among Hindus, it was the god Indra who threw the lightning bolt creating the mushroom"** (think satori – lightning).

ED's view of the mushroom reflects her view of satori, where overnight a new entity springs into being:

> The Mushroom is the Elf of Plants –
> At Evening, it is not –
> At Morning, in a Truffled Hut
> It stop upon a Spot

In the morning, when you first see the mushroom in your yard, it looks as if it had always been there:

> As if it tarried always
> And yet its whole Career
> Is shorter than a Snake's Delay
> And fleeter than a Tare –

It seems to come & go in an instant, like "a Snake's delay," striking up from the ground in an instant.

---

*   Difficult Questions, Easy Answers, 96.
** Ibid, 97.

'Tis Vegetation's Juggler –
The Germ of Alibi –
Doth like a Bubble antedate
And like a Bubble, hie –

The toadstool, among Nature's vegetation, is the juggler/conjurer who seems to manipulate reality: it is <u>al-ibi</u> (as they say in Latin), the secret source, or Germ, of "elsewhere": now you see it, now you don't. Like satori it comes & goes, & one is pleased to have it "intermit":

I feel as if the Grass was pleased
To have it intermit –
This surreptitious scion
Of summer's circumspect.

It is an intermittent surprise, like ED herself, who comes & goes "surreptitiously," by stealth, as she says in P-1596:

Few, yet enough,
Enough is One –
To that ethereal throng
Have not each one of us the right
To stealthily belong?

The mushroom is the scion –offspring, shoot—"Of Summer's circumspect." "Circumspect," from L. <u>circumspicio,</u> "to look around, seek, wait for," is used here with a verbal force (cf. "retrospect," "introspect," "prospect"). Of the seasons of the year, summer is the season of all-encompassing growth, when Nature looks everywhere, seeks everywhere, & awaits every possibility. The mushroom is always her least expected form:

Had Nature any supple Face
Or could she one contemn –
Had Nature an Apostate –
That Mushroom – it is Him!

Like the bat, that "renegade mammal," the mushroom appears to be an apostate, renouncing the natural order of things as recognized by the farmer. If there were any growth in Nature that you could credit with a "supple Face," it would be the toadstool, readily adaptable to any habitat. Such is the face of satori, our original face, the one we had before our parents were born. It is not conceived, gestated, & born according to any recognized order of Nature.

755

No Bobolink – reverse His Singing
When the only Tree
Ever He minded occupying
By the Farmer be –

Clove to the Root –
His Spacious Future –
Best Horizon – gone –
Whose Music be His
Only Anodyne –
Brave Bobolink -

IRREVERSIBLE SINGING

ED, like many another transcendentalist, spontaneously recognizes the so-called Doctrine of Signatures, the experience of sensing spiritual "signs" in the Book of Nature. She recognizes herself as it were in certain natural phenomena, such as the symbiosis of bee/rose, or the hidden threat/promise of the volcano. In the present poem the bobolink, seen as an "outsider," assumes this surrogacy.

ED's readers recognize the bobolink as a bird especially close to her heart. Her detailed portrait of this bird in P-1279 ("The Way to know the Bobolink") includes details uniquely applicable to her own character:

> Of Sentiments seditious
> Amenable to Law –
> As Heresies of Transport
> Or Puck's Apostacy.
>
> Extrinsic to Attention
> Too intimate with Joy –
> He compliments existence
> Until allured away

Throughout her life ED's experiences of satori were "Transports" revealing heresies, & creating "Sentiments seditious." Her sentiments are amenable to the Law of Nature, making her a puckish apostate vis-à-vis church law.

Like ED, the bobolink "compliments existence / Until allured away." ED remains the witness/poet of human existence until allured away by the temporal demands of Dickinson.

The bobolink is characterized here as the sorcerer of the Meadow:

> How nullified the Meadow -
> Her Sorcerer withdrawn!

Dickinson herself, when she sits down to write poetry, "withdraws," & becomes the sorcerer, our Juggler of P-1170:

> Behold our spacious Citizen
> Unto a Juggler turned –

These considerations are relevant to the present poem, which concerns the bobolink's tenacity, the way it follows its instinctual nature regardless of outward circumstances:

> No Bobolink – reverse His Singing
> When the only Tree
> Ever He minded occupying
> By the Farmer be –
> Clove to the Root –

In the bobolink ED recognized her "apostacy" (P-1279), her determination to obey the demands of the Psyche, Mother Nature in human form. Her enterprise was a secret labor that contradicted the premise of her conventional life in Amherst. The severe limitation of a provincial ego-identity threatened to deny her a place to sing, like the tree denied to the bobolink:

> His Spacious Future –
> Best Horizon – gone –

ED's secret enterprise was her "Spacious Future," her "Best Horizon" — but outward circumstances, however discouraging, could not possibly make her "reverse her singing," as she says in P-613 ("They shut me up in Prose"):

> They might as wise have lodged a Bird
> For Treason – in the Pound –

Her "treason" is of a piece with her "apostasy" & her "heresy."

The war between ego & non-ego, between Dickinson & ED, was traumatic, & chronically so. The poetry was an anodyne, as with the bobolink:

> Whose music be his
> Only Anodyne –
> Brave Bobolink –

The joy of obeying her instinctual, creative needs alleviated the pain of being out of synch, of disappointing the expectations of loved ones, of not sharing the cultural values of the people sharing Dickinson's household.

1645

The ditch is dear to the Drunken man
For is it not his Bed –
His Advocate – his Edifice?
How safe his fallen Head
In her disheveled Sanctity –
Above him is the sky –
Oblivion bending over him
And Honor leagues away.

THE TOWN DRUNK

ED's thoughts on the "Drunken man" are of special interest, because she relates to him in her own private way.

Like other transcendentalists, ED associates ego-transcendence both with orgasm & with intoxication; satori is a "divine" form of these, "The divine intoxication" of P-76. P-214 is her best-known description of this:

> I taste a liquor never brewed –
> From Tankards scooped in Pearl –
> Not all the Vats upon the Rhine
> Yield such an Alcohol!

ED's thoughts on the drunkard are extrapolated from her own experience with the intoxication of ego-loss. Intoxication & orgasm are psychological states that share with satori the fact of egolessness. It is true that there are egocentric fornicators & drinkers seeking to enhance ego by fornicating & drinking; but ED is not interested in pursuing ego-enhancement – hence she focuses on the drunkard lying in a ditch, & not on the raving alcoholic full of ego-passions.

The drunkard in a ditch is an outcast, the town drunkard; & it is no great stretch to think of ED as the Town Drunk in a transcendental sense. In P-838 she says,

> Impossibility, like Wine
> Exhilarates the Man
> Who tastes it;

Enlightenment is the "Impossibility" of which she speaks, for so it seems to the egocentric mind: like the miracle, it is an impossibility come true.

The ditch, says ED, is the drunkard's bed, advocate, & edifice. Her use of "advocate" is a kind of Shakespearean joke: the ditch "supports" him. It is the Ground of his being, where "his fallen Head" is safe "In her disheveled Sanctity." ED's use of "her" suggests her involvement with this metaphor of the drunken man.

"Disheveled Sanctity" is the heart of this poem. "Disheveled" means "bareheaded, with disordered hair," & evokes the notion of "letting your hair down," acting naturally, without ego-defense. "Sanctity" is the key word that connects ego-transcendence with drunkenness, for the realm of the Holy is the realm surpassing ego. Ego is disheveled when transcended.

ED's last three lines here describe a person in the state of nirvana, or ego-extinction:

> Above him is the sky —
> Oblivion bending over him
> And Honor leagues away.

"Honor" is an ego-invention, self-worth based on what others think of you. Satori is the sky of oblivion bending over you — same as the River Lethe, as ED says P-1730:

> "Lethe" in my flower,
> Of which they who drink
> In the fadeless orchards
> Hear the bobolink!

To drink the waters of Lethe is to become drunk with satori, "above you only sky," & others' opinions leagues away.

IV. EGO-TRANSCENDENCE AS HERESY

ED, HERETIC

ED's oeuvre tells the story of her life as it unfolded in terms of her sense of identity, her sense of who she was, or might be. She had grown up with the understanding that she was a person called Emily Dickinson but then she was struck by the lightning of ego-transcendence.

The Christian worldview is based on the assumption that the ego-self is a solid reality. It can survive death, in the form of an ego-soul morally responsible to a personal God. "You," in this enduring form, will be rewarded or punished, according to your spiritual track record. When satori strikes ego dead, however, all the church business is wiped out: goodbye ego-soul, goodbye Heaven & Hell. Enlightenment has replaced theology. ED regarded this as her Coronation, as she declares, in P-356:

> The Day that I was crowned
> Was like the other Days –
> Until the Coronation came –
> And then – 'twas Otherwise -

There upon (she goes on to say), "I rose, & all was plain." Not only was the dharma plain to her; it was also plain to her that she had been reborn as a heretic. This was her "appalling Secret." She did not discuss it with anyone, but it became the basis of her mission in life, to go on record as witness/poet of the dharma.

413

I never felt at Home – Below –
And in the Handsome Skies
I shall not feel at Home – I know –
I don't like Paradise –

Because it's /Sunday – all the time –
And Recess – never comes –
And Eden'll be so lonesome
Bright Wednesday Afternoons –

If God could make a visit –
Or ever took a Nap –
So not to see us – but they say
Himself – a Telescope

Perennial beholds us –
Myself would run away
From Him – & Holy Ghost – & All –
But there's the "Judgment Day"!

THE AFTERLIFE

Him, & Holy Ghost, & All

> My idea of heaven is, eating paté
> de foie gras to the sound of trumpets.
>
> Sydney Smith (1771-1845)

ED's awareness of the dharma meant rejection of egocentric values, including the notion of permanent happiness in a heaven tailored to the tastes of the Christian ego-self.

> I never felt at Home – Below –
> And in the Handsome Skies
> I shall not feel at Home – I know -
> I don't like Paradise –

There is little difference between the idea of ego-happiness here below, & its counterpart "in the Handsome Skies." ED had no "home below," because hers was the "Heart that accepted / Homelessness for Home" (P-1010). Her path in life is as described in the opening lines of the Tao Te Ching:

> The paths men take are named.
> My path, ever emergent,
> cannot be named.

In the present poem Paradise, the Christian afterlife, is an object of satire, as in P-215:

> What is – "Paradise" –
> Who live there –
> Are they "Farmers" –
> Do they "hoe" –
> Do they know that this is "Amherst" –
> And that I – am coming – too –

The Christian heaven is an egocentric Paradise where "it's Sunday – all the time" (line 5). Transcendentalists cannot help but notice how Christians distinguish between the workweek & the Sabbath; during six days one lives profanely, then on Sunday dresses up & sits solemnly in church, in the religious mode, like children at Sunday school. Heaven naturally comes to be imagined as a perpetual Sunday school, with never any recess. In P-324 ED remarks on this "religious mode":

> Some keep the Sabbath going to Church -
> I keep it, staying at Home –
> With a Bobolink for a Chorister –
> And an Orchard, for a Dome –

ED recognizes that Christians (regardless of their theologians) treat God as the Man Upstairs, the celestial Santa Claus who's "keeping a list & checking it twice. Gonna find out who's naughty & nice." In the present satire the Man Upstairs "Perennial beholds us" with His Cosmic Telescope.

ED fantasizes that in Heaven she "would run away" from the Holy Trinity, nonchalantly called "Him – & Holy Ghost –& All." But then she reminds herself that she may never even get into

Heaven, may never even have to deal with the Sunday School teacher Upstairs; after all, "there's the 'Judgment Day'!"

If Emily Dickinson is sentenced to Hell, God help the rest of us!

P-413

Addendum: Where is Home?

> ...existence strays / Homeless at home.
> (from P-1573)

> heart that proposed as Heart that accepted
> Homelessness, for Home –
> (from P-1010)

"Home" is essential to both ego & non-ego. Emily Dickinson's home was the Homestead in Amherst, & was the center of attachment to her daily life as a member of the socially prominent Dickinson family.

"Home," in the transcendentalist sense, refers to the Present Moment, the "place" where we were all born to begin with, our Original Mind. Thich Nhat Hahn, exiled Vietnamese Zen monk, says, when asked about his "homelessness," "… although I have not been able to go back to Vietnam, I am not in pain, I do not suffer, because I have found my true home."* This monk founded a Zen center called Plum Village; he says,

> Every time we listen to the sound of the bell in...
> Plum Village, we silently recite this poem; 'I listen, I
> listen, this wonderful sound brings me back to my

---

* <u>Buddhadarma</u> (Spring 2005), 13.

true home. Where is our true home...? [It] is life; our true home is the present moment, whatever is happening right here & right now.*

Pema Chodron, a prominent Buddhist author/teacher, refers to the ordinary meaning of "home" when she says that "becoming a Buddhist is about becoming homeless.**

ED, a prominent Buddhist poet of Amherst, says (aware of Emily Dickinson's strong attachment to the Homestead) "I never felt at Home — Below." Not only that; she adds,

> And in the Handsome Skies
> I shall not feel at Home – I know –
> I don't like Paradise –

She says this, or course, since the Christian Heaven is an egocentric projection, like "eating pate de foie gras to the sound of trumpets." Chrisitan theology posits the Heaven / Hell dialectic, but popular belief ignores Hell. Churchgoing Christians —especially the charismatics—believe that they are already "saved," & that they will go to Heaven. All you have to do is be born again.

ED grew up aware of the tent revival meetings popular in her day, meetings where the people went to be "saved." So "Paradise" was only an Amherst Upstairs, created by the Man Upstairs.

---

* Ibid. Thich Nhat Hanh is widely known as the founder of the Engaged Buddhism peace movement, which became active in the 1960s, & continues unabated to the present day.

** Tricycle (Fall, 1993), 18..

1303

Not One by Heaven defrauded stay –
Although he seem to steal
He restitutes in some sweet way
Secreted in his will -

THE AFTERLIFE

NOT TO BE DENIED

The epigram is one form taken by what I call ED's "interactive style." Her terseness requires the reader to bring an informed frame of reference in order to extrapolate the text. This frame of reference is, of course, a familiarity with the semantics of non-ego reality.

The epigram, in general, by reason of its terseness, typically demands that one read between the lines. To appreciate the wit of Oscar Wilde's epigrams you must share his urbane detachment (e.g., "One must have a heart of stone to read the death of little Nell without laughing.") ED's epigrams typically depend upon a key word or idea unique to her own experience, as in the present poem:

> Not One by Heaven defrauded stay –
> Although he seem to steal
> He restitutes in some sweet way
> Secreted in his will –

What you make of this depends upon what you think she means by being "defrauded by Heaven."

Throughout her poetry ED uses "heaven' in both the religious sense & in the transcendentalist sense. According to Christian doctrine, "Heaven" means the Afterlife, God's reward to the faithful. According to the transcendentalist experience of satori, "heaven' is the bliss of cosmic awareness, or nirvana.

ED, in growing up, found herself "defrauded by Heaven," in the sense that the Christian notion of Heaven turned out to be a cheat, a pious fairy tale. They had tried to foist it off on her, but satori exposed the lie: there is no solid, unchanging ego-self, any more than there is a solid, unchanging rainbow.

The notion of being defrauded by religious doctrine is clear in P-1630 ("As from the earth the light Balloon"), where the spontaneous, soaring flight of the balloon awakens a sense of indignation,

> As a Bird
> Defrauded of its song.

This is the same bird that appears in P-1574:

> No ladder needs the bird but skies
> To situate its wings
> Nor any leader's grim baton
> Arraigns it as it sings.

The church elders have little tolerance for the transcendentalist who experiences ego-transcendence outside the boundaries of their grim orthodoxy: in fact, theocracies have usually regarded heresy as a capital crime.

When ED says, "Not One by Heaven defrauded stay," she means "one who realizes that he has been defrauded." This means ED herself, of course, since it is her own personal experience that validates the epigram. This is what gives special meaning to "stay": "Not One by heaven defrauded stay." She means "stay in the church." During ED's adolescence people were forever trying to get her to stay in the church, to make a commitment; but she early had her own experience of "heaven," & so would not be persuaded.

ED here apologizes for the heretic, who seems "to steal":

> Although he seem to steal
> He restitutes in some sweet way

"Steal," in this context, means "to appropriate to oneself, without permission." ED had stolen Heaven!

But then she spent the rest of her life "restituting" "in some sweet way / Secreted in [her] will." I take "will" to mean "the power of control over one's actions" (Merriam-Webster), as in P-361:

> What I can do – I will –
> Though it be little as a Daffodil –
> That I cannot – must be
> Unknown to possibility –

ED's creative genius furnishes the power "secreted" in her unshakeable will to create poetry precisely as she wills it to be done.

1399

Perhaps they do not go so far
As we who stay, suppose —
Perhaps come closer, for the lapse
Of their corporeal clothes —

It may be know so certainly
How short we have to fear
That comprehension antedates
And estimates us there -

THE AFTERLIFE

THE RENDEZVOUS OF LIGHT(S)

Here ED muses on the notion of transcendent consciousness before & after death. Many a transcendentalist, including Plato, has regarded death as what ED, in P-1564, calls a "Rendezvous of Light," referring to an appointed meeting of earthly human consciousness & cosmic consciousness.*

According to popular religious belief, when people die, they "go somewhere." ED, demurring, opines,

> Perhaps they do not go so far
> As we who stay, suppose –
> Perhaps come closer, for the lapse
> Of their corporeal clothes –

This idea is suggested by the obvious fact revealed by satori: if unconditioned awareness can be experienced before death, & if death is a Rendezvous with that same awareness, then the descent comes "closer," closer than ever, since we then share the same naked awareness – they having cast off their "corporeal clothes."

ED's second stanza is syntactically loose:

---

* The two are one, hence the singular "Light," not the plural "Lights." This is comparable to the singular "Monarch" in P-642: "And since we're mutual Monarch."

It may be know so certainly
How short we have fear
That comprehension antedates
And estimates us there –

The last two lines describe ego-transcendence as an experience that "antedates comprehension" by giving us a rough preview of what lies beyond the grave. I take "It" to mean "That comprehension": our transcendent comprehension perhaps know[s] so certainly how briefly we have to fear passage beyond physical death.

ED's use of "short" suggests an intuition of what the Tibetan Buddhists call the bardos, the "in-between states" connecting one's death & rebirth.* Buddhists recognize that satori, "That comprehension," occurs in the bardo between inbreath & outbreath, whereupon one "Inhales the different dawn" (P-87) – not "a different dawn," but "the different dawn." This bardo is indeed "short" – & so may be the bardo between death here, & consciousness "there."

---

* The title Bardo thodol, known to us as the Tibetan Book of the Dead, means "Liberation through Hearing in the In-between State" (The Shambhala Dictionary of Buddhism & Zen).

1491

The road to Paradise is plain,
And holds scarce one.
Not that it is not firm
But we presume
A Dimpled Road
Is more preferred.
The Belles of Paradise are few –
Not me – nor you –
But unsuspected things –
Mines have no Wings.

THE AFTERLIFE

THE ROAD TO PARADISE

Again we should note ED's two meanings for "Paradise": (1) the Christian Heaven, & (2) ego-transcendence, also called "ecstasy," "bliss," "exhilaration," "rapture," "glory," etc., throughout her poetry.

The Christian Paradise is something her neighbors believe in; her own Paradise is the actual experience of the higher Self. In the first line here she declares, "The Road to Paradise is plain." The first thing you are apt to remark about enlightened mind is how <u>obvious</u> it is ("Why hadn't I seen this before?").

In the second line she says that this Road "holds scarce one." Enlightened awareness is Oneness with the world reality, Unity, with no solution of continuity. You are a bird in the air, a fish in the water. You are One, not Two. "Two" is ego's way of thinking — what the Buddhists call "dual mind": "I/it," "I/you." Buddha Mind holds One, just so.

In lines 4-6 ED alludes to the common notion of Paradise which is entertained by church people. "We" (line 4) —the community at large—presume a "Dimpled Road," meaning all smiles.* Heaven is joyful, while Hell is misery. The Beautiful People (Belles) may go to the Christian Heaven, but the Belles of ego-transcendence are few — certainly they are "Not me — nor you" (line 8).**

---

* For this meaning of "dimple," see poems 347, 351, 476, 514, & 559.

** This may be a quote from the song "Some Folks," by Stephen Foster (1826-64), which ED could well have known. In it Foster contrasts the attitude of some folks with "us": "Some folks scrimp & save, to buy themselves a grace, but that's not me nor you."

In sum, the Christian Paradise is up above; the Paradise of ego-transcendence is in the bowels of Mother Nature, like a precious mine — a familiar ED metaphor, as in P-466, where she calls herself the "Prince of Mines." For the transcendentalist the alternative to "Heaven above" is not "Hell down there," but the Here & Now of non-ego awareness, liberated from theological hypotheses.

560

It knew no lapse, nor Diminution –
But large – serene –
Burned on – until through Dissolution –
It failed from Men –

I could not deem these Planetary forces
Annulled –
But suffered an Exchange of Territory –
Or World -

CHRISTIAN MYTH

AN EXCHANGE OF WORLD

To awaken to cosmic awareness is to know that non-ego reality is the Way Things Are, the Tao, forever constant. Civilizations rise & fall, as ego-illusions are created & demolished. Victory & defeat are their yang & their yin.

While civilizations can last for centuries, traditional tribal cultures endure for many millennia. This is because these are not founded on ego-illusions or ego-mastery of Nature & control of external events. They exist within the dharma, & their habitat is who they are, as embodied in their totems & rites of passage.

Civilization marks the emergence of ego-awareness from the dharma-centric home on earth called Eden. The opposites are born; people become aware of good & evil, of virtue & sign, I "in here," & the world "out there."

Such is the background for the present poem, one of ED's many "It" poems:

> It knew no lapse, nor Diminution –
> But large – serene –
> Burned on – until through Dissolution –
> It failed from Men –

Christian doctrine has it that an angry creator God expelled Adam & Eve from Eden because they had sinned against Him. The primitive alpha male ego rejoices in its own self-awareness — so much so that it projects itself as the creator of the universe, able to tyrannize, to make the rules, to punish the transgressors & to reward the obedient. It projects itself as the Man Upstairs.

Adam & Eve's original sin is traditionally known as their lapsus, their "fault"; hence their honeymoon in Eden is known as "prelapsarian." In the present poem ED, with her sound knowledge of these matters, cannily critiques the Bible story when she says that the dharma "knew no lapse." That is to say, the non-ego utopia called dharma was not involved in the lapsus described in Genesis.

Early civilization sees primitive alpha males repressing dharma-centric awareness, but the dharma

> Burned on – until through Dissolution –
> It failed from Men –

The triumph of ego within the economy of Psyche "dissolved" the presence of the dharma in the consciousness of men; it "failed from Men," meaning that it became repressed, & ceased to exist in the mind of civilized man.*

So when the lapsus occurred, the dharma "knew no lapse." ED, when she awakened, realized this instantly, as do all who awaken:

> I could not deem these Planetary forces
> Annulled –
> But suffered an Exchange of Territory –
> Or World –

Cosmic awareness is awareness of "Planetary forces," forces that were never affected, much less "annulled" by the emergence of ego-consciousness. What happened was simply a new, ego-based ontology, "an Exchange of Territory – Or World." This

---

* The construction "to fail from" appears in Job 14:11, "as the waters fail from the sea." The OED defines this as "become exhausted, come to an end."

"Exchange," from non-ego to ego, is redressed by satori, which reverses the direction, taking one from ego to non-ego. This is what ED, in P-593, calls "Conversion of the Mind":

> I could not have defined the change –
> Conversion of the Mind
> Like Sanctifying in the Soul –
> Is witnessed – not explained –

Satori, then, is an Exchange of World whereupon one sees the obvious, that the Tao could never be affected by the vicissitudes of human history. We can't change the Way Things Are; we can only wake up.

673

The Love a Life can show Below
Is but a filament, I know,
Of that diviner thing
That faints upon the face of Noon —
And smites the Tinder in the Sun —
And hinders Gabriel's Wing —

'Tis this — in Music — hints & sways —
And far abroad on Summer days —
Distils uncertain pain —
'Tis this enamors in the East —
And tints the Transit in the West
With harrowing Iodine —

'Tis this — invites — appalls — endows —
Flits — glimmers — proves — dissolves —
Returns — suggests — convicts — enchants —
Then — flings in Paradise —

CHRISTIAN MYTH

THE ANNUNCIATION

This is an impetuous love poem, an Ode to Joy — meaning the Joy of Buddha Mind, the Great Union, the Oneness. Gone is the separation between the self & Nature, as if by magic: suddenly you are free.

"Joy" —& its many synonyms—abound in ED's transcendent discourse, as in P-1382:

> In many & reportless places
> We feel a Joy —
> Reportless, also, but sincere as Nature
> Or Deity —

Transcendent Joy is "The joy that has no stem nor core, / Nor seed that we can sow" [P-1744].* It is the Joy of liberation from the ego-self, & in the present poem ED makes a clear distinction between egocentric love & transcendent love:

> The Love a Life can show Below
> Is but a filament, I know,
> Of that diviner thing

"Diviner" is an example of what I call the "transcendentalist comparative" [favored also by Thoreau], as in P-383:

---

* For "Joy" in the transcendent sense, see also poems 1404, 1430, 1434, 1465, 1580, 1679, & 1717.

233

> Exhilaration – is within –
> There can no Outer Wine
> So royally intoxicate
> As that diviner Brand

The intoxicating wine of satori is "wine of a higher sort."

"Filament" is used in the sense of "thread," as "thread in the fabric of life." Human love, then, is part of the diviner love

> That faints upon the face of Noon –
> And smites the Tinder in the Sun –
> And hinders Gabriel's Wing –

"Noon" is one of ED's many metaphors for satori, the locus classicus being P-1056, where unconditioned awareness is a "Zone" where "Consciousness – is – Noon."

I call this poem a paean, because the Greek paean was originally a hymn of praise addressed to Apollo, the Sun God. Transcendent Oneness, or Love, is Enlightenment, for it "smites the Tinder in the Sun" [line 5].

Line 6 of this poem is curious. Why should Enlightenment hinder Gabriel's Wing?

Gabriel is best known as the angel of the Annunciation (Luke 1:26-38), & his most famous words to Mary are doubtless, "blessed art thou among women." This Annunciation featuring Gabriel, in the context of ED's discourse, takes on a special meaning; for ED, as a woman who vouchsafed satori, must have thought often about the singular fact that she, seemingly an inmate in an unforgiving patriarchal household, had been vouchsafed a vision of liberation. The Annunciation is a crucial event in the myth of how Christianity came to be the patriarchal Religion of Choice. Gabriel told Mary that she was blessed among women, because she had been chosen to be the mother of God, the great Patriarch in the Sky — the one we Americans call the Man Upstairs.

ED was very aware that satori liberated her from the patriarchal monopoly of "reality." This is why she says, most justly, that it "hinders Gabriel's Wing." With satori, the patriarchy won't fly.

The rest of this paean is a delirious litany to Becoming. Once you awaken from the static dream of ego that "thinks, therefore it is," you find yourself in the Only Dance There Is (as Ram Dass puts it): "'Tis this — in Music — hints & sways."

The poem concludes with a manic litany of love:

'Tis this — invites — appalls — endows —
Flits — glimmers — proves — dissolves —
Returns — suggests — convicts — enchants —
Then — flings in Paradise —

"Appalls" echoes P-281, where ED says, "Tis so appalling — it exhilarates." The last four lines of the present poem are richly passionate, & you are free to punctuate as you please. In an early poem on satori (P-42) ED experimented with punctuation: "A Day! Help! Help! Another Day!" Then she evidently decided that there is no reason for punctuation. If the reader understands what she is saying, he or she will supply the punctuation as needed. This is an example of what I call ED's interactive style.

The last line of this poem appeals to me for its colloquial flavor; "Then — flings in Paradise." Satori does all the things ED says: it "invites," "appalls," "endows," "flits," "glimmers," etc. But then — it throws in Paradise as an added attraction!

171

Wait till the Majesty of Death
Invests so mean a brow!
Almost a powdered Footman
Might dare to touch it now!

Wait till in Everlasting Robes
That Democrat is dressed,
Then prate about "Preferment" —
And "Station," & the rest!

Around this quiet Courtier
Obsequious Angels wait!
Full royal is his Retinue!
Full purple is his state!

A Lord, might dare to lift the Hat
To such a Modest Clay
Since that My Lord, "the Lord of Lords"
Receives unblushingly!

EGOCENTRISM

WHEN THE ROLL IS CALLED UP YONDER, I'LL BE THERE!

ED's apparent satire of Christian belief is actually a satire of our unanimous belief in the reality of the ego-self. The experience of ego-transcendence reveals a "not-self" (anicca, as the Buddhists say). One sees that all contingent phenomena are illusory, like the rainbow, contingent upon a certain condition of sunlight & water droplets. The ego-self is the most profoundly contingent phenomenon of all. The social being that I regard as "me" depends, first of all, on the time & place of birth. Then come gender assignment, language, ethnicity, religious & political identity, & all the rest. Had a Muscovite couple adopted me as an infant, all that would be different, & I would now be "somebody else." Satori makes this glaringly obvious.

The traditional theme called the Dance of Death describes Death as the Great Leveler; one's social status vanishes. But our religious idea of death is based on the belief in an "ego-soul" that survives death intact, & so goes to its eternal reward or punishment in the afterlife. Theologians may tergiversate about this, but the churchgoers do not. The following statement by a current superstar (George Strait) is typical of the mainstream belief:

> I'm a religious person. I honestly believe we will see
> each other in heaven someday.*

---

*   Interview in <u>USA Weekend</u> (Jan. 19-21, 2007).

Strait, like his fans, sees this as "religious" belief — but the religious belief itself is rooted in egocentrism. Egocentrism comes first, then religion, because ego invents its own salvation.

This is an important point in the context of ED's apparent satire of religion. One thinks of P-215 ("What is---'Paradise' "), or P-98 ("one dignity delays for all"), concerning funerals:

> How pomp surpassing ermine
> When simple You, & I,
> Present our meek escutcheon
> And claim the rank to die!

The present poem is a meditation on our virtually ineradicable belief in the ego-self as a permanent reality. ED begins boldly by stating that Death is a "Majesty":

> Wait till the Majesty of Death
> Invests so mean a brow!
> Almost a powdered Footman
> Might dare to touch it now!

According to the Christian doctrine, the ego-soul is glorified on high. Heaven is like the court of Louis XIV, the Sun King, & we blessed ego-souls are the aristocracy.

In the second stanza of the present poem ED stresses the fact that Heaven is a form of "Preferment":

> Wait till in Everlasting Robes
> That Democrat is dressed,
> Then prate about "Preferment" —
> And "Station," & the rest!

On Judgment Day God separates the sheep from the goats, just as portrayed by Dante. Good egos go to Heaven, bad egos go to Hell.

When we die, we are instantly waited upon by "Obsequious Angels":

> Around this quiet Courtier
> Obsequious Angels wait!
> Full royal is his Retinue!
> Full purple is his state!

At last ego gets full recognition for being what it always knew it was.

In the final stanza ED suggests the contradiction between our two different uses of "Lord":

> A Lord, might dare to lift the Hat
> To such a Modest Clay
> Since that My Lord, "the Lord of Lords"
> Receives unblushingly!

We have always used social caste as the basis for metaphors describing God: King, Prince, Lord. ED is struck by the fact that "the Lord of Lords" is not embarrassed to receive as equals all these dignitaries, these lords that have suddenly been resurrected from "Modest Clay." If ED herself has seen through the illusion of the ego-self, is not our Lord embarrassed to credit that same illusion?

475

Doom is the House without the Door –
'Tis entered from the Sun –
And then the Ladder's thrown away,
Because Escape – is done –

'Tis varied by the Dream
Of what they do outside –
Where Squirrels play – & Berries die –
And Hemlocks – bow – to God –

He deposes Doom
Who hath suffered him –
(From P-1181)

EGOCENTRISM

WHO IS A LIFER?

This poem, & P-590 ("did you ever stand in a Cavern's Mouth"), written at about the same time (c.1862), treat the same theme; existential imprisonment in the form of the ego-self, described as a dark cave in P-590, & here as a "House of Doom." In both poems one is in a dark interior, shut away from the light of the Sun. In the present poem, this House of Doom is accessed by a ladder, not a door.

The ego-self is formed from childhood on by the process called "socialization," whereby the tot is weaned from natural (non-ego) mind, so as to grow into the predetermined, customary limits ordained by social traditions. These limitations may be fairly flexible in ancient tribal societies, where the ego-self remains relatively vague throughout life. In a highly evolved urban society the ego-self becomes highly specialized & straitlaced, particularly from the transcendentalist's viewpoint (not to mention that of the teenager).

The growing child does not simply "walk through the door," into the cultural domicile of the elders; he or she must be "brung up" step by step, rung by rung, as if climbing the ladder of social selfhood.* So this domicile is "the House of Doom," & once

---

* These successive steps of child development have been documented in detail by Jean Piaget (1896-1980), the Swiss behaviorist.

241

the child is securely ensconced, "Escape — is done" (line 3). Life within this House is "varied by the Dream / Of what they do outside," "they" being the inhabitants of the natural world with its round of seasons.

The reference to the Hemlocks bowing to God (last line) is double-edged; for while it evokes the tree (fir or spruce), it also takes one to the locus classicus, the death of Socrates. The Squirrels playing & the Berries dying evokes the seasons (spring, winter); but Hemlocks bowing to God countermand society's condemnation of Socrates. Liberty of conscience & liberty of consciousness are beyond the strictures of any social establishment.

The epigraph from P-1181 is crucial to ED's outlook:

> He deposes Doom
> Who hath suffered him —

Virtually no one ever questions the validity of the ego-self as an ontological reality. Most of us simply take it for granted. This is our Doom. If you do not see that "you" (ego-self) is quite arbitrary, contingent upon time & place, then you are doomed to be that "you." If, however, one experiences the ego-self as a form of oppression (like racism or sexism), then one will suffer it, not accept it. If you have this attitude, then you have already "deposed" it; it is no longer the undisputed king of Psyche. At that point in one's individuation, the House of Doom may begin to look like the House of the Rising Sun.

1196

To make Routine a Stimulus
Remember it can cease –
Capacity to Terminate
Is a Specific Grace –
Of retrospect the Arrow
That power to repair
Departed with the Torment
Become, alas, more fair –

EGOCENTRISM

> Before enlightenment, fetching water & chopping wood;
> after enlightenment, fetching water & chopping wood.
> Zen saying

PAIN & SUFFERING, ALAS!

Routine, whether ego-driven or not, is daily life, precious because it is impermanent, as ED says in P-1741:

> That it will never come again
> Is what makes life so sweet.

The capacity to transcend the sense of routine as boredom: this is a "Specific Grace," namely, the Arrow of retrospect [line 5]. This "retrospect," or "looking back," reveals your original, pre-ego mind before it became any ego-self. Ego-transcendence is just such a revelation – the experience of Pure Mind, unimpaired, uncrippled, but the emergence of ego. ED sees here that Buddha Mind is "That power to repair" the unhappy ego-self, characterized by duhkah, "suffering." "Life is duhkah," says the First Noble Truth.

ED lived in a Christian community, & so was intimately familiar with how they treat suffering. They learn early on to accept suffering, or "Torment," as a Christian ordeal, like that of Job. Christ himself suffered for our sins, & suffering, they think, is an opportunity to test their piety. Alas!

Enlightenment reveals the emptiness of the ego-self, &

therefore the emptiness of ego-suffering to which we are attached. As faithful Christians grow into accepting the reality of ego, they see suffering as "fair," because it has a divine purpose. Alas!

A "natural-born" transcendentalist like ED, once she has experienced the exhilaration of ego-transcendence, cannot "un-initiate" herself & return to business as usual. She may continue to live "as if" she were plain old Emily Dickinson, pretending to believe in that illusion (& no one the wiser), but, as she says in P-1741,

> Believing what we don't believe
> Does not exhilarate.

Nevertheless, with eyes opened by enlightenment, she cannot experience "routine" anymore. The Zen saying quoted above is modified:

> Before enlightenment, routine;
> After enlightenment, routine – not!

Though the present poem is eight lines long, ED does not divide it into two quatrains, as she frequently does; hence I read line 5 as a continuation of lines 1-4. Rephrasing a bit, & adding punctuation, I understand these lines as follows:

> To turn Routine into a Stimulus,
> Remember that it can cease;
> The capacity to terminate "routine"
> Is a Specific Grace,
> namely, the Arrow of Retrospect.

Ego-transcendence reveals the emptiness of the ego-self, & therefore the emptiness of ego-suffering. As faithful Christians grow into accepting the reality of the ego-self, they become convinced that suffering has a divine purpose. Alas!

915

Faith – is the Pierless Bridge
Supporting what We see
Unto the Scene that We do not –
Too slender for the eye

It bears the Soul as bold
As it were rocked in Steel
With Arms of steel at either side –
It joins – behind the Veil

To what, could We presume
The Bridge would cease to be
To Our far, vacillating Feet
A first Necessity.

FAITH

> Now faith is the substance of things hoped for
> the evidence of things not seen.
> Heb. 11:1

> The faith that stands on authority is not faith.
> Ralph Waldo Emerson

THE TWO KINDS OF FAITH

The transcendentalist has faith —confidence, trust—in Mother Nature, because Psyche is Mother Nature in human form. This is to say that the transcendentalist has faith in our instinctual nature, & not in the arbitrary cultural authority imposed by the collective ego.

The present poem deals with theistic faith, the religion that the parents foist "Upon an unsuspecting Heir" (P-1090).

In the first stanza ED rephrases the well-known epigram of St. Paul, quoted above: theistic faith is the evidence of things "Too slender for the eye" (line 4). That is a poor excuse for evidence!

The second stanza describes the true believers afoot on their Pierless Bridge leading to what lies "behind the Veil." Her expression "Pierless Bridge" deserves commentary, because it is likely satirical. A pierless bridge is one without any physical support (pier); but if you read this poem aloud, every listener would hear "peerless." Every true believer believes that his or her religion is a peerless bridge to heaven; but there is nothing on earth to support any theology.

Now what lies "behind the Veil"? For the transcendentalists (e.g., the Buddhists) what lies behind the Veil is actually "A first Necessity" (last line). The Veil is the curtain of dual mind which hides Reality. Ego believes that it is separate from Mother Nature, & that when the body dies, ego will go to heaven. But Enlightenment is the "first Necessity" of human life, because it is the original grasp of Reality with which we were born. Enlightenment requires no bridge leading up yonder; it makes us know that we are already "there" — which is Here & Now.

377

To lose one's faith — surpass
The loss of an Estate —
Because Estates can be
Replenished — faith cannot —

Inherited with Life —
Belief — but once — can be —
Annihilate a single clause —
And Being's — Beggary —

FAITH

We shall not cease from exploration
And the end of all our exploring
Will be to arrive where we started
And know the place for the first time.
                    -- T. S. Eliot, "Little Gidding"

DISENCHANTING THE SOUL

This poem deals with the natural faith in instinct with which we are born, by contrast to the blind faith expected of churchgoers, the "Pierless Bridge" of P-915, just examined. Now ED speaks of losing one's natural faith as a calamitous event, described in P-1451 as "disenchanting the soul." This is the price we pay for becoming "socialized," & saddled with an illusory, ad hoc ego-self. It is the loss of our original faith (confidence) in the Oneness of Reality, a faith we are all born with, "Inherited with Life" (line 5). We are soon weaned, learning to regard Reality as dual — "I" vs. "World." ED says that this is worse than a material loss, because "Estates can be / Replenished."

Of course ED knows whereof she speaks (she speaks no other way), & recognizes that she herself never did lose the faith she "inherited with Life." But she also saw the society of people around her as having permanently lost their innate faith in the Oneness of Life. They wear a "Contented — Beggar's face" (P-359), & will never do otherwise.

This poem reminds one that ED was unaware of formal meditation as practiced in the East, especially by the Buddhists. In her day Americans were not aware of meditation traditions & techniques practiced throughout Asia, & Buddhists were considered to be idolatrous pagans. Today, a well-known American Buddhist center flourishes in Barre, Massachusetts, only a few miles east of Amherst. These adepts are all well aware that the loss of our "original face" does indeed reduce human life to "Being's — Beggary."

476

I meant to have but modest needs –
Such as Content – & Heaven –
Within my income – these could lie
And Life & I – keep even –

But since the last – included both –
It would suffice my Prayer
But just for One – to stipulate –
And Grace would grant the Pair –

And so – upon this wise – I prayed –
Great Spirit – give to me
A Heaven not so large as Yours,
But large enough – for me –

A Smile suffused Jehovah's face –
The Cherubim – withdrew –
Grave Saints stole out to look at me –
And showed their dimples – too –

I left the Place, with all my might –
I threw my Prayer away –
The Quiet Ages picked it up –
And Judgment – twinkled – too –

That one so honest – be extant –
It take the Tale for true –
That "Whatsoever Ye shall ask –
Itself be given You" –

But I, grown shrewder – scan the Skies
With a suspicious Air –
As Children – swindled for the first
All Swindlers – be – infer -

PRAYER

REMINISCING

ED thinks back to the early years, before she awakened, when her worldview was conventional: happiness consisted of Christian contentment. She had no spiritual ambition to live "beyond her income"; she would spend only what was afforded her by the community, just like everyone else. But in line 3 she inserts the ambiguous verb "lie":

> I meant to have but modest needs –
> Such as Content – & Heaven –
> Within my income – these could lie
> And Life & I – keep even –

At the time, she thought that conventional contentment could "lie," meaning "remain undisturbed"; & so her life would pass without spiritual incident. But of course at the end of this poem she speaks of being "swindled," so this suggests a second connotation for "lie": conventional contentment could <u>lie to her</u>, & she, like everyone else, was willing to accept the lie.

In stanza two ED describes how she accepted the role played by religion:

> But since the last – included both –
> It would suffice my Prayer
> But just for One – to stipulate –
> And grace would grant the Pair –

The "last" (latter)—Heaven—"included both": as the faithful are always telling us, without faith in God you will never know "true contentment" — which is a self-fulfilling prophecy. There is no reason to doubt it so long as you remain ensconced in the reality of the ego-self. For the faithful, this is a foretaste of the Heaven to come. So young Emily prayed, in the Christian manner:

> And so – upon this wise – I prayed –
> Great Spirit – Give to me
> A Heaven not so large as Yours,
> But large enough – for me –

ED's reference to Jehovah & the "Grave Saints" in stanza four makes it clear that she is thinking of the Old Testament:

> A Smile suffused Jehovah's face –
> The Cherubim – withdrew –
> Grave Saints stole out to look at me –
> And showed their dimples – too –

The intermediates made way for Jehovah Himself, & she imagined that the dignified old prophets were beaming their approval.

In stanza five ED appears to describe the "transvaluation of values" occasioned by enlightenment:

> I left the Place, with all my might –
> I threw my Prayer away –
> The Quiet Ages picked it up –
> And Judgment – twinkled – to –

Conventional Christian prayer supposes a communion between ego & God, just as ED has been describing all along; but something happened. She "left the Place." What "Place" is this? I would say, as our modern usage has it, "the place where she was at." She discarded the conventional notion of prayer, & the conventional notion of "Judgment," at the same time. Judgment was no longer <u>dies irae</u>, for its power to terrorize had been drained away, once there was no longer any ego-self left to be terrorized.

In stanza six ED turns to the New Testament, Matthew 7:7: "Ask, & it shall be given you."

> That one so honest – be extant –
> It take the Tale for true –
>
> That "Whatsoever Ye shall ask –
> Itself be given You" –

Jesus, "extant" among the faithful, speaks honestly – who could doubt it? But the last stanza states ED's skepticism:

> But I, grown shrewder – scan the Skies
> With a suspicious Air –
> As Children – swindled for the first
> All Swindlers – be – infer –

She was a skeptic by temperament, in any case; but ego-transcendence demonstrated that all scriptures are "Tales," hearsay. Any transcendentalist who reads ego-transcendence as the revelation of a theology is fraudulent, perverting the truth for ego-ambition.

564

My period had come for Prayer –
No other art – would do –
My Tactics missed a rudiment –
Creator – Was it you?

God grows above – so those who pray
Horizons – must ascend –
And so I stepped upon the North
To see this Curious Friend –

His House was not – no sign had He –
By Chimney – nor by Door
Could I infer his Residence –
Vast Prairies of Air

Unbroken by a Settler –
Were all that I could see –
Infinitude – Had'st Thou no Face
That I might look on Thee?

The Silence condescended –
Creation stopped – for Me –
But awed beyond my errand –
I worshipped – did not "pray" –

PRAYER

LEARNING TO PRAY

ED's spiritual evolution naturally entailed a new understanding of Prayer. As a girl she had been taught to say her prayers, as she recalls in P-576:

> I prayed, at first, a little Girl,
> Because they told me to –
> But stopped, when qualified to guess
> How prayer would feel – to me –

P-1539 is her evolved, transcendent version of the standard bedtime prayer:

> Now I lay thee down to Sleep –
> I pray the Lord thy Dust to keep –
> And if thou live before thou wake –
> I pray the Lord thy Soul to make –

In various poems ED treats of the contrast between prayer as a petition from ego to God, & prayer as a form of transcendent meditation, or mindfulness [e.g., poems 103, 376, 476, 1751). The present poem is a detailed consideration of these two modes of praying.

The first stanza describes prayer in the form of ego-transcendence:

My period had come for Prayer –
No other Art – would do –
My Tactics missed a rudiment –
Creator – Was it you?

Satori had become an off-&-on occurrence, & here ED says "My period had come for Prayer," which appears to be suggested by the association of "period" with the cyclic occurrence of menstruation – which can be very erratic, as I have been told.*

In line 2 ED calls her form of meditation an "Art," as in P-326 ("I cannot dance upon my Toes"):

Nor any know I know the art
I mention – easy – Here –

Here I take "art" in the sense described in Merriam-Webster: "a personal, un-analyzable creative power (the <u>art</u> of choosing the right word)." This art has become the rudiment of her enterprise.

In line 3 ED speaks of "Tactics," which evokes P-320, where she contrasts ego-play to transcendent play:

We play at Paste –
Till qualified, for Pearl –
Then, drop the Paste –
And deem ourself a fool –

The Shapes – though – were similar –
And our new Hands
Learned *Gem*-Tactics –
Practicing *Sands* –

_____

* The OED's earliest citation of this use of "period" is 1822.

259

Her "Gem-Tactics" correspond to the "Tactics" of the present poem.

In line 4 ED addresses the Creator god, the object of all ego-prayers, the one described in P-437:

> Prayer is the little implement
> Through which Men reach
> Where Presence – is denied them.
> They fling their Speech
>
> By mean of it – in God's Ear –
> If then He hear –
> This sums the Apparatus
> Comprised in Prayer –

The Creator God is, of course, the "rudiment" of ego-prayer. Ego-transcendence taught ED that her new mode of prayer had discarded this basic element. The fact that she addresses this now superfluous entity is a nice psychological touch, a backward look to something fading from view.*

Stanza two concerns ED's growing detachment from the prayerful habits of her earliest years:

> God grows above – so those who pray
> Horizons – must ascend –
> And so I stepped upon the North
> To see this Curious Friend –

The Christian faithful think of God as a Higher Being in Heaven. This Being "grows," as ED says, coming to realize that the

---

* I recall speaking thus to God when, as a child, I decided that I was an atheist. I made my final prayer, my adieu, saying, "God, I don't believe in you anymore, so good-bye."

Christian Creator God is a myth or legend that continually grows
& changes, as He is adapted to local requirements.

Stanza three plays satirically upon the notion of God's Heaven
as a "lace":

> His House was not – no sign had He –
> By Chimney – not by Door
> Could I infer his Residence –

ED goes on to describe the Empty Mind of satori:

> Vast Prairies of Air
> Unbroken by a Settler –
> Were all that I could see –

This is what she calls "Wastes" in P-458:

> Like Eyes that looked on Wastes –
> Incredulous of Ought
> But Blank – & steady Wilderness –
> Diversified by Night –
>
> Just Infinites of Nought –
> As far as it could see –

Just a moment ago she addressed God; now she addresses
"Infinite":

> Infinitude – Had'st Thou no Face
> That I might look on Thee?
>
> The Silence condescended –

"Condescended" here means "to behave as if on equal terms,

without losing the air of superiority" (my tailored definition). Satori creates a Silence of Mind that is intimate & awesome at the same time. In line 5 ED says, "God grows above"; but here, in the final stanza, she says, with a fine irony, that Creation "stopped":

> Creation stopped – for Me –
> But awed beyond my errand –
> I worshipped – did not "pray" –

She has attained an Absolute, & she is "awed beyond my errand," she says.

This is the "errand" of which she speaks in P-95; when egocentric people talk of nature,

> They bear no other errand,
> And I, no other prayer.

Conventional people have no "mission" when they speak of nature; ED herself has an absorbing errand/mission, to record her "prayers,' (I call them sutras) in a form finally available to us. Therefore she always "worshipped – did not 'pray'," she says, putting "pray" in quotation marks; "I did not 'pray' (as they say)."

423

The Months have ends – the Years – a knot –
No Power can untie
To stretch a little further
A Skein of Misery –

The Earth lays back these tired lives
In her mysterious Drawers –
Too tenderly, that any doubt
An ultimate Repose –

The manner of the Children –
Who weary of the Day –
Themselves – the noisy Plaything
They cannot put away –

RESURRECTION

THE NOISY PLAYTHING

ED here lays special emphasis on what the Buddhists call the first noble Truth: life is suffering (duhkah). This is not her only reference to the subject; in P-1168 she says,

> As old as Woe –
> How old is that?
> Some eighteen thousand years –
> As old as Bliss
> How old is that
> They are of equal years
>
> Together chiefest they are found
> But seldom side by side
> From neither of them tho' he try
> Can Human nature hide

Recognizing ED's use of "Bliss" meaning satori, or nirvana (ego-extinction), we understand here that egocentric life is Woe, while liberation is Bliss (as the Third Noble Truth states).

In the present poem the first stanza states the inevitability of suffering:

> The Months have ends – the Years – a knot –
> No Power can untie
> To stretch a little further
> A Skein of Misery –

This inevitability is, as she says, a function of life lived in clock time. The "Skein of Misery" is so completely part of the fabric of ego-life that its presence could hardly be increased or exaggerated — especially when one thinks of all our ongoing social catastrophes (ED was writing during our Civil War).

The second stanza may be understood in two different ways:

> The Earth lays back these tired lives
> In her mysterious Drawers –
> Too tenderly, that any doubt
> An ultimate Repose -

The graveyard is filled with "mysterious Drawers," where the dead find "An ultimate Repose." "Ultimate Repose" may be read as a variant of the cliché "final resting place," but —apart from the fact that ED does not deal in clichés—the term here takes its meaning from context: the funeral rites are attributed to Mother Earth, not to society. Earth, not we, is the one who "lays back these tired lives." She does it as a loving mother would put her baby in its cradle, with all the tenderness in the world, ensuring that it should rest undisturbed. Such are the "tired lives" of earthlings. Their burial is a matter of dust to dust, & their repose is ultimate. "Ultimate" means not only "final," but also "primary," "fundamental" — hence "irreversible." The dead cannot arise again, cannot become undead (there are no zombies), because Earth Herself has taken them back into Herself.

Egocentric lives are lived in clock time —months & years—& this is the milieu of the ego-self. Beyond clock time ego has no existence, nor can it be eternalized in the Christian heaven. This sense of an ego-identity dependent upon clock time is what formal meditators seek to transcend. They recognize ego as a "noisy Plaything / They cannot put away"—"monkey mind," they call it, just as ED calls it a "puppet," in P-287:

A Clock stopped –
Not the Mantel's –
Geneva's farthest skill
Can't put the puppet bowing –
That just now dangled still –

Meditators are typically people who grow "Weary of Day," life in ego's clock time, on ego's terms; but when they practice meditation they confront the hard fact that they are saddled with a "noisy Plaything They cannot put away." At some point Mother Earth puts it away for us, once & for all.

515

No Crowd that has occurred
Exhibit – I suppose
That General Attendance
That Resurrection – does –

Circumference be full –
The long restricted Grave
Assert her Vital Privilege –
The Dust – connect – & live –

On Atoms – features place –
All multitudes that were
Efface in the Comparison –
As Suns – dissolve a star –

Solemnity – prevail –
Its Individual Doom
Possess each separate Consciousness –
August – Absorbed – Numb –

What Duplicate – exist –
What Parallel can be –
Of the Significance of This –
To Universe – & Me?

RESURRECTION

DOOMSDAY

This is one of ED's more trenchant satirical poems concerning the popular Christian notion of an afterlife; here, the resurrection, the rising again to life of all the human dead, prior to the final judgment. Previously, in P-215, ED has satirized the notion of ego-souls going to Heaven:

> What is – "Paradise" –
> Who live there –
> Are they "Farmers" –
> Do they "hoe" –

[For our discussion of this poem, see <u>Solitary Prowess</u>, 94-96.]

Satori is called "ego-transcendence," since it reveals the non-existence of any solid ego-self. The ego-self is contingent upon time & place, & can no more survive intact than can a rainbow die & go to Heaven.

Any attempt to visualize resurrection as a reunion of ego-identity with a glorified physical body ("corporealization") soon reveals self-evident contradictions; & in the present poem, ED immediately betrays her skepticism with the expression "I suppose":

> No Crowd that has occurred
> Exhibit – I suppose
> That General Attendance
> That Resurrection – does –

The resurrection, as believers envision it, requires the "General Attendance" – <u>bodily</u> attendance—of all the human beings who have lived on earth since the Creation. This will require all the clay that Mother Earth can spare.

In the second stanza ED begins to picture the scene:

> Circumference be full –
> The long restricted Grave
> Assert her Vital Privilege –
> The Dust – connect – & live –

For ED, "circumference" is a generic term meaning "field of awareness," including the "field" of which a spectator is aware, as an arena or the stage.* The "restricted Grave" is now revealed as endowed with "Vital Privilege," for the atoms of dust "[re] connect – & live." This is the dust of P-813:

> This quiet Dust was Gentlemen & Ladies
> And Lads & Girls –
> Was laughter & ability & Sighing
> And Frocks & Curls.

Lo, they rise again, as gentlemen & ladies. This is the dust that [re]places features on atoms:

> On Atoms – features place –
> All Multitudes that were
> Efface in the Comparison –
> As Suns – dissolve a star –

The antecedent of "Efface" is "Grave" [line 6]: the Grave "Assert her Vital Privilege," & "Efface" & previous notion of "Multitudes," as sunlight "dissolves" starlight.

---

* See <u>Solitary Prowess</u>, "Mandala," 166-181

In stanza four is found ED's dramatization of Resurrection which appears to reflect the revivalist preaching of her day:

> Solemnity – prevail –
> Its Individual Doom
> Possess each separate Consciousness –
> August – Absorbed – Numb –

Judgment Day is Doomsday, & "each separate Consciousness" expects to be "cast in the lake of fire" as threatened in Rev. 20:15.*

In the final stanza ED poses her rhetorical question:

> What Duplicate – exist –
> What Parallel can be –
> Of the Significance of This –
> To Universe – & Me?

Here she reveals herself as an "outsider": "what has this apocalyptic vision got to do with the "Universe – & Me?"

Ego-transcendence has revealed that the higher Self is cosmic consciousness which ED calls the "Universe – & ME." The Christian notion of an eternatl ego-self is irrelevant to the dharma; it does not signify, it offers no parallel to the Tao, the Way Things Are.

---

* Strangely enough, in P-1273 ("That sacred Closet when you sweep - / Entitled 'Memory'") ED refers to the dust of memories as "August": "August the Dust of that Domain." In our present poem, the resurrected august dust is benumbed by memories of its sinful self.

313

I should have been too glad, I see –
Too lifted – for the scant degree
Of Life's penurious round –
My little Circuit would have shamed
This new Circumference – have blamed –
The homelier time behind.

I should have been too saved – I see –
Too rescued - Fear too dim to me
That I could spell the Prayer
I knew so perfect – yesterday –
That Scalding One – Sabachthani –
Recited fluent – here –

Earth would have been too much – I see –
And Heaven – Not enough for me –
I should have had the Joy
Without the Fear – to justify –
The Palm – without the Calvary –
So Savior – Crucify –

Defeat – whets Victory – they say –
The Reefs – in old Gethsemane –
Endear the Coast – beyond!
'Tis Beggars – Banquets – can define –
'Tis Parching – vitalizes Wine –
"Faith" bleats – to understand!

SALVATION

BEFORE & AFTER

In <u>Solitary Prowess</u> we have discussed at length ED's use of "circuit" & "circumference" as meaning one's "circle of awareness" (pp.174 et sqq.). In the present poem Dickinson's conventional "little Circuit" (line 5), that "homelier time" (line 6) contrasts with ED's "new Circumference" (line 5). Assessing her initial enthusiasm for this enlightened awareness, she remarks amusingly that if her naïve enthusiasm has persisted, she would have been "too saved," "too rescued" (lines 7-8). Such is the arrogance of the neophyte, thrilled with a sense of obvious superiority.

In this second stanza ED ponders her dutiful "religious" attitude of yore. Like a catechumen, she memorized standard biblical passages, as (for example), Matthew's version of the Crucifixion, including the Seven Last Words ("My God, why hast thou forsaken me?"), the "Eli, lama Sabachthani?" of 27:46. Here the pious Christian may ponder the depth of the Sacrifice ensuring that God would never forsake His people.

In stanza three ED states her realization that without Liberation she would have "had the Joy / Without the Fear — to justify / The Palm." Earthly life, as experienced by the ego-identity, "would have been too much"; while (given her skeptical temperament) Pie in the Sky would have been "not enough." She realizes now that the pious Christian has the joy of feeling "saved," without the fear of ego-loss. The transcendentalist braves the fear of ego-loss, as ED says in P-1360:

> I sued the News – yet feared – the News
> That such a Realm could be –
> "The House not made with Hands" it was –
> Thrown open wide to me –

Pious Christians simply rejoice because ego has been "saved" for eternity. He (of she) gets the "palm" (victory) without Calvary (sacrifice of the ego-self). Christian theology assures us that death is not a problem, because ego is eternal. Satori shows us that ego is a passing fancy, sublimely ignorant of the dharma.

Line 19 reads, "Defeat – whets Victory – they say." This echoes P-67:

> Not one of all the purple Host
> Who took the Flag today
> Can tell the definition
> So clear of Victory
>
> As he defeated – dying –
> On whose forbidden ear
> The distant strains of triumph
> Burst agonized & clear!

No one senses more the meaning of victory than the one who suffers the agony of defeat. It was in the Garden of "old Gethsemane" (line 20) where Jesus, as a suffering human being, agonized & was arrested as a capital offender. This "defeat" --according to Christian doctrine-- assured us of our safe arrival in Heaven.

Adducing another instance of "allopathic" consciousness-raising, ED says "'Tis Beggars – Banquets – can define" (line 22). In P-119 she has said similarly,

> Talk with prudence to a Beggar
> Of "Potosi," & the mines!
> Reverently, to the Hungry
> Of your viands, & your wines!

In the same manner, "'Tis Parching – vitalizes Wine" (line 23). These examples of "allopathic consciousness-raising" culminate in the final line: "'Faith' bleats – to understand!"

"Faith" (in quotation marks is the "blind faith" required of the flock. The sheep "bleats" to understand the meaning of salvation, & is ready & willing to follow someone else's lead (cf. the Wiffenpoof Song: " We are poor little sheep who have gone astray, baa, baa, baa"). But ED is not of the flock, nor is she a follower of anyone touting a "revealed truth." She has experienced non-ego for herself. She was "parched," & now, she says, in P-214,

> I taste a liquor never brewed –
> From Tankards scooped in Pearl –
> Not all the Vats upon the Rhine
> Yield such an Alcohol!

325

Of Tribulation, these are They,
Denoted by the White –
The Spangled Gowns, a lesser Rank
Of Victors –designate –

All these – did conquer –
But the ones who overcame most times –
Wear nothing commoner than Snow –
No Ornament, but Palms –

Surrender – is a sort unknown –
On this superior soil –
Defeat – an outgrown Anguish –
Remembered, as the Mile

Our panting Ankle barely passed –
When Night devoured the Road –
But we – stood whispering in the House –
But we – stood whispering in the House –
And all we said – was "Saved"!

SALVATION

SALVATION, TRANSCENDENTALIST STYLE

In transcendentalist language (such as that of Buddhism) salvation is equivalent to ego-transcendence, when the Higher Self is "saved" (rescued) from the claustrophobic confinement of the illusory ego-identity. By contrast with Christianity, you cannot be saved by anyone else. As the Zen saying puts it, "If you do not get it from yourself, where will you go for it?" You become your own savior, by transcending from the little "you" to the Great You, the <u>maha-atman</u>.

ED sometimes refers to transcendence as an "escape," as in P-1347, "Escape is such a thankful Word." In that same poem she makes a point of saying of the Great Escape:

> 'Tis not to sight the savior –
> It is to be the saved –
> And that is why I lay my Head
> Upon this trusty word –

In P-160 ED describes a Near Escape:

> Just lost, when I was saved!
> Just felt the world go by!
> Just girt me for the onset with Eternity,
> When breath blew back,
> And on the other side
> I heard recede the disappointed tide!

Such is the salvation of the present poem, which ends with the exclamation "Saved!": "And all we said — was 'Saved'!"

Of the present poem Sewall says that it presents "the paradox of victory in defeat in a way perhaps a military man... would understand" (557). It is true that ED uses a military metaphor here (she was living during our Civil War), but it is needful to see this as a metaphor, precisely, & not simply as a historical reference. No military man would likely understand her metaphor.

This poem begins with a reference to the white flag of surrender. The victors, designated by ceremonial robes, are "a lesser Rank" (line 3). "Lesser Rank" is an example of the "transcendental comparative," where the profane meaning of a word is cast aside, in favor of a transcendent meaning. In the "Conclusion" to <u>Walden</u> (for example), Thoreau refers to transcendence as "an older, a newer, & purer wine, of a more glorious vintage." In this same spirit "a lesser Rank / Of Victors" refers to egocentric victors, as (for example) the post-election ins & outs. The "Greater Rank" of victors ("Victors of a higher order," as Thoreau would say) are the unfettered minds of the Enlightened, "wearing" nothing commoner than the seasons of the year (snow, palm trees), like the classical haiku poets.

Unlike Emily Dickinson, ED stands on the "superior soil" of ego-transcendence (another transcendental comparative). When one is "saved" by Buddha Mind (just as the Buddha was), then defeat becomes "an outgrown Anguish" (line 11). This is the tribulation that one has outgrown. We have previously noted her reference to this in P-563:

> I do not doubt the self I was
> Was competent to me —
> But something awkward in the fit —
> Proves that — outgrown — I see —

When one becomes enlightened, the old egocentric duality ("I" vs. "World") is merely remembered as a time "When Night devoured the Road" (line 14). "Night" is in contrast to "Light," as in Enlightenment: "I recall walking the Road of Life in darkness,

> But we – stood whispering in the House –
> And all we said – was "Saved"!

Traveling the Road of Life is in contrast to the House of Psyche, where one simply stands alive. Ego-transcendence revives the bond with Psyche, the bond with which one was born.

696

Their Height in Heaven comforts not –
Their Glory – nought to me –
'Twas best imperfect – as it was –
I'm finite – I can't see –

The House of Supposition –
The glimmering Frontier that
Skirts the Acres of perhaps –
To Me – shows insecure –

The Wealth I had – contented me –
If 'twas a meaner size –
Then I had counted it until
It pleased my narrow Eyes –

Better than larger values –
That show however true –
This timid life of Evidence
Keeps pleading – "I don't know."

SOUL

ZEN EVIDENCE

For the conventional Christian churchgoer, belief in life after death is the basic comfort. Christian doctrine solves the problem of death by assuring us that we can survive in Heaven; to the believer this means, in effect, survival of the ego-identity in the form of "ego-soul." As the Baptist hymn proclaims, "When the roll is called up Yonder, I'll be there!" The traditional Negro spiritual dwells on this belief as a final source of comfort in the face of a lifetime of slavery. Redemption not only from sin, but from suffering, is the strongest suit of the Christian faith: I will survive death & suffer no more.

In the present poem ED records her reaction to such an appeal. Speaking of the departed souls presumed to dwell in Heaven, she says,

> Their Height in Heaven comforts not –
> Their Glory – nought to me –
> 'Twas best imperfect – as it was –
> I'm finite – I can't see –

Egocentric life on earth is "imperfect," being finite; but it is here & now; &, in any case, the issue is not death; the issue is ego.

In the second stanza ED goes on to describe the faithful as attending worship in "The House of Supposition":

> The House of Supposition –
> The Glimmering Frontier that
> Skirts the Acres of Perhaps –
> To Me – shows insecure –

The "Glimmering Frontier" separating this life from the afterlife may be crossed hypothetically – but this requires "Acres of Perhaps." The most seriously flawed "Supposition" assumes the existence of a permanent ego-self which, upon one's death, magically becomes an "ego-soul."

In stanza three ED, playing the born-againer, remains skeptical of the spiritual gain promised:

> The Wealth I had – contented me –
> If 'twas a meaner size –
> Then I had counted it until
> It pleased my narrow Eyes –

ED, as Emily Dickinson, may have estimated her spiritual wealth with "narrow Eyes," but in the end she recognizes her gut preference:

> Better than larger values –
> That show however true –
> This timid life of Evidence
> Keeps pleading – "I don't know."

Given ED's fondness for legalese, "plead" should be understood thus, "to argue a case."

ED, as a hard-core empiricist, will not credit hearsay doctrine. She lives, as she modestly phrases it, a "timid life of Evidence." What she has not experienced personally remains unknown. Theology is The House of Supposition. P-1770 is the locus classicus of ED's empiricism:

Experiment escorts us last –
His pungent company
Will not allow an Axiom
An Opportunity

"Experiment" (i.e., experience, L. experimentum) is the court of last appeal, & its down-to-earth pungency will brook no theoretical contradiction, however "axiomatic." Religious doctrine regarded as accepted wisdom is hearsay, & no amount of scripture can make it otherwise. ED's attitude is akin to that of Zen Buddhism, which eschews scripture & doctrine, demanding verification by personal experience.

836

Truth – is as old as God –
His Twin identity
And will endure as long as He
A Co-Eternity –

And perish on the Day
Himself is borne away
From Mansion of the Universe
A lifeless Deity.

THEISM

> There is no god higher than Truth.
> -- Mahatma Gandhi

THE CO-ETERNITY

When Gandhi says, "There is no god..." he is clearly referring to different religious doctrines equating the Truth with their particular theology. This has political consequences which, for Gandhi, is the point of his statement. "Mahatma" is maha-atman, "Great Self," or "Great Breath" (spiritus).

The Higher Self is atheistic, & realizes that all theistic religions see "God" in their own image. Their God is a projection of the collective ego. There is no good reason to choose this theology over that one: this much is abundantly clear to Atman Mind. Theologians are intelligent men who get carried away by their ego-intellect.

This, I believe, is at the root of ED's satirical bent. She was reared in a strict & pious patriarchal atmosphere, &, having experienced the emptiness of her own ego-self, could hardly have not regarded the patriarchal ego as equally empty. By temperament she was subversive, not outwardly rebellious, like Susan B. Anthony, her senior by ten years. To ED, Enlightenment was not politics.

In the present poem ED's first line contrasts with Gandhi's remark concerning Truth & God. ED clearly does not have in mind a theistic god. Rather, "God" is a synonym for "Truth" —they are "Twins," meaning that they come from the same womb. They are a "Co-Eternity" — not "God the Father & God the Son," but "God the Truth & Truth the God."

This Co-Eternity will perish on the Day

> Himself is borne away
> From Mansion of the Universe
> A lifeless Deity.

Which is to say, "Never!" ("That'll be the day!") The only one who could abscond with the truth ("bear it away") would be an all-powerful patriarchal God or Jehovah. Theistic religions appear to do this, to kidnap the Truth from our cosmic Mansion & turn it into "A lifeless Deity." But satori always recovers —or rediscovers—the Truth. You awaken & exclaim, "There is no god higher than Truth!"

357

God is a distant – stately Lover –
Woos, as He states us – by His Son –
Verily, a Vicarious Courtship –
"Miles", & "Priscilla", were such an One –

But, lest the Soul – like fair "Priscilla"
Choose the Envoy – & spurn the Groom –
Vouches, with hyperbolic archness –
"Miles", & "John Alden" were Synonym –

THEISM

SPEAK FOR YOURSELF, JESUS

Transcendentalists easily experience ego-transcendence as the visit of a lover (e.g., Song of Solomon, Rumi). God is wooing a Soul. ED, in a clever, "arch" variation of this theme, uses as a metaphor the story of the courtship of Miles Standish — how he wooed "'fair' Priscilla" vicariously, sending John Alden as his envoy. After Alden had delivered the message, Priscilla famously replied, "Speak for yourself, John Alden."*

In the present poem this becomes a transcendentalist metaphor: Standish is God, Alden is Christ, & ED is Priscilla. ED says that if she were Priscilla, she would not "Choose the Envoy — & spurn the Groom." She says this with irony, assuring us "with hyperbolic archness," that Standish & Alden are "Synonym," i.e., two different names for the same thing.

Christians assert this very fact, or course — that God the Father & God the Son are Synonym; but Christians do not assert this ironically. They assert it with the greatest seriousness. So ED's "archness" gives a different meaning to the "Holy Synonym."

Readers of the Dickinson biographies are familiar with the fact that family & friends pressured young Emily to make a public avowel of faith, which was customary in the church. She resisted, of course; her transcendentalist temperament transcended doctrine. Like the Buddhists, ED experienced ego-transcendence as an

---

* This is according to the apocryphal story related by Longfellow, in his poem, "The Courtship of Miles Standish: (1858).

experience, not a belief system. Within the metaphor Standish/ Alden/Priscilla, ED's Soul is Priscilla, who <u>already knows</u> whom she loves. She is a skeptic by temperament, & so she notes ironically, "with hyperbolic archness," that Standish & Alden are Synonym. Any transcendentalist knows this: you & Buddha Mind are One, as much so as any other transcendentalist, including Jesus Christ. Christians are too literal about the Father/Son business. Christ was not <u>the</u> son of God, he was <u>a</u> son of Buddha Mind, just as ED was <u>a</u> daughter of Buddha Mind. Buddha Mind has as many daughters & sons as there are transcendentalists.

513

Like Flowers, that heard the news of Dews,
But never deemed the dripping prize
Awaited their – low Brows –

Or Bees – that thought the Summer's name
Some rumor of Delirium,
No Summer – could – for Them –

Or Arctic Creatures, dimly stirred –
By Tropic Hint – some Travelled Bird
Imported to the Wood –

Or Wind's bright signal to the Ear –
Making that homely, & severe,
Contented, known, before –

The Heaven – unexpected come,
To Lives that thought the Worshipping
A too presumptuous Psalm –

THEISM

THE HEAVEN UNEXPECTED COME

This poem is a panegyric written to celebrate the gift of satori, "The Heaven — unexpected come." Satori is a gift to humankind ("Lives," line 14), & not just to ED. As the Buddha himself recognized, if any one of us can experience ego-transcendence, then everyone can: it is the human condition, not a special gift bestowed upon elite prophets for the purpose of founding or confirming a religious doctrine.

Several similes lead up to the final stanza, all referring to natural phenomena that happen "unexpectedly," because the recipient is completely unaware that such a thing can be. ED begins by suggesting an obvious reference to established religion:

> Like Flowers, that heard the news of Dews,
> But never deemed the dripping prize
> Awaited their — low Brows —

The churchgoing faithful are taught that they, the flock, are led by a shepherd especially favored — Heaven's Favorite Son as it were—who heard God speaking privately to him, telling him to found a church & to begin converting people. Every Sunday morning the congregation hears the "news," the gospel, never deeming that they, the "low Brows," could possibly experience any such Revelation on their own.*

---

* The noun "lowbrow" did not come into popular usage until early twentieth century, according to Random House Unabridged, so ED's reference here is probably not intended satirically.

In the second stanza ED suggests another spiritual possibility: "Delirium."

> Or Bees – that thought the Summer's name
> Some rumor of Delirium
> No Summer – could – for Them –

Nonbelievers may regard divine revelations as the ravings of a lunatic such as Joseph Smith (for example), who founded the Mormon Church in 1830, the year of Dickinson's birth (that was a vintage year).

In stanza three ED provides a more personal reference:

> Or Arctic Creatures, dimly stirred –
> By Tropic Hint – some Travelled Bird
> Imported to the Wood –

By "Arctic" I understand "Arctic regions," like the Russian taiga, a subarctic forest (or "Wood") beginning where the tundra ends. I say that the reference is "more personal," because Dickinson, as we have noted, has already likened her awakened Self to an "Arctic flower" (P-180).

Civilizations—especially Occidental civilizations—are formidably egocentric, meaning that the people are "Arctic Creatures": their hearts are frozen. Nature is to be conquered & exploited, not espoused as our Better Half.

Stanza four depicts satori as the Wind / Spiritus:

> Or Wind's bright signal to the Ear –
> Making that homely, & severe,
> Contented, known, before –

"Wind's bright signal to the Ear" is one of ED's many <u>inspired</u> descriptions of Spiritus. Here she says that before satori ever occurred, Spiritus had already allowed her to intuit its presence. The Wind's signal to the ear created a secret understanding long before the Heaven unexpected came: it made "that" known (lines 11-12), "that" being what she has been talking about all along. It was "homely," "severe," & "contented."

"Homely" & "severe" mean "plain," by contrast with the elaborate church doctrine & ritual. It was also "contented," at one with its habitat, like the sacred contented cows of India.

But then comes the bolt out of the blue;

> The Heaven – unexpected come,
> To Lives that thought the Worshipping
> A too presumptuous Psalm –

A few skeptical churchgoers –like Dickinson, for example—cannot help but regard Sunday worship as "presumptuous," based on the presumption that this particular church has a monopoly on Truth. Such is the experience of the heretics fortunate enough to be in tune already with a reality beyond ego, unbeknownst to themselves.

1112

That this should feel the need of Death
The same as those that lived
Is such a Feat of Irony
As never was – achieved –

Not satisfied to ape the Great
In his simplicity
The small must die, as well as He –
Oh the Audacity –

THEISM

APING THE GREAT

ED has a number of "It" poems, in which she does not specify what "It" means. These poems are among her most "cryptic," but they yield their meaning readily enough when you understand that the nameless "It" is Buddha Mind, the Tao — of which Lao Tzu says, in the Tao Te Ching, #25, "Impossible to name this insight. I just call it The Way." Similarly, for ED this insight is simply "It."* In the present poem "It" appears as "This": This is It.**

It is truly mind-blowing (as the hippies put it) to experience cosmic awareness yourself, & then to realize that you have shared in the dharma with the most celebrated transcendentalists in world history, the ones whose experience has led to the founding of great religions. Yet, there is no getting around it, as the Buddhist adepts have always recognized: the great prophets are not an elite few selected by God as exclusive recipients of His Messages. Ancient civilizations have always recognized the priestly caste as the middlemen purveying God to us humble, undeserving citizens. The Buddha, however, cautioned against this elitism. He said, "Don't take my word for what I say: follow the Path & experience it for yourself."

Meanwhile, back in nineteenth-century New England, ED comes to recognize that the Bible is a biased account of Jesus as a

---

* For examples, see poems 420, 904, 1301, 1344, 1360, 1700.

** Fans of Alan Watts will recognize this as one of his titles.

dharma teacher; for his followers make him out to be literally the one & only Son of God. Enlightenment teaches you, however —if you are willing to let this happen—that your core experience of the dharma is identical with that of Jesus. All the rest is hearsay dignified with the name "theology."

The present poem is a meditation on this matter:

> That this should feel the need of death
> The same as those that lived
> Is such a Feat of Irony
> As never was – achieved –

This is to say that "This"—your own ego-transcendence—requires ego-death, by definition. It doesn't occur to churchgoers that they themselves can experience what Jesus experienced, & never mind all the biased "interpretations" (these came much later). ED's point in the present poem is that her sense of sharing in Jesus' core experience is "audacious"; how dare she think that she has experienced what Jesus experienced? This sense of "audacity" is "a Feat of Irony," because, after all, Jesus the man was a humble person, to begin with. His followers exalted him, turned him into God the Creator. Isn't it ironic that I, a humble member of the Christian community, should suddenly discover that Jesus & I are dharma equals? He didn't "save" me; we were both saved from the self by transcending it.

In the second stanza ED rephrases her point:

> Not satisfied to ape the Great
> In his simplicity
> The small must die, as well as He –
> Oh the Audacity –

Back in line 2 ED says "those"; now she uses the singular; when you experience satori you "ape the Great / In his simplicity."

ED was unaware that the Buddha had addressed the "irony" of which she speaks. He said, in effect, "I am nothing special, just like you; we are all Buddhas by virtue of our humanity, our ability to awaken, to be liberated." No one can "save" anybody else. It is as the Zen Buddhists say: "If you do not get It from yourself, where will you go for It?" To awaken in the dharma, "you' must let the ego-self die, just as Jesus did. Oh the Audacity!

1244

The Butterfly's Assumption Gown
In Chrysoprase Apartments hung
This afternoon put on –

How condescending to descend
And be of Buttercups the friend
In a New England Town –

1651

A Word made Flesh is seldom
And tremblingly partook
Nor then perhaps reported
But have I not mistook
Each one of us has tasted
With ecstasies of stealth
The very food debated
To our specific strength –

A Word that breathes distinctly
Has not the power to die
Cohesive as the Spirit
It may expire if He –
"Made Flesh & dwelt among us"
Could condescension be
Like this consent of Language
This loved Philology.

THEISM

ASSUMPTION & CONDESCENSION: THE CONSENT OF LANGUAGE

What ED calls the "consent of Language" (P-1651, line 15) is well illustrated by the two ideas featured in P-1244, "assumption" & "condescension." They both have a literal & a figurative meaning which she exploits with her particular kind of wordplay allowed by her "loved Philology" (P-1651, last line).

In P-1244 a butterfly, emerging from the chrysalis, dons an "Assumption Gown," & "condescending" descends upon the buttercups in Amherst. (The expression "Chrysoprase Apartments"—green foliage—sounds like an implied pun on "chrysalis."*)

"Assumption" is, of course, a term in Roman Catholic doctrine, according to which the Mother of God was "assumed," or taken up bodily, into heaven after her death. In English the common noun "assumption" has only the figurative meaning, not the "alien" Catholic one. In Spanish asunción usually means Asunción, as in the place name Asunción, Paraguay; our "assumption" is rendered suposición.) In her Butterfly Poem ED, by "consent of language," makes a non-Christian, "heathen" reference to the insect's Assumption Gown.

---

* "Chrysalis" & "Cocoon" are images of ego-transcendence. In P-1099, "My Cocoon tightens – Colors tease," ED applies this metaphor to herself. It is relevant here to recall Emanuel Swedenborg, the legendary transcendentalist of 18th-century Sweden: the Swedenborg Foundation publishes a journal called Chrysalis.

Her use of "condescending" [line 4] echoes "Assumption": the butterfly rises to heaven as a Higher Form of life, & then "condescends" to descend, i.e., nobly deigns to come down from on High.

P-1651, "A Word made Flesh," again, by Consent of Language, makes use of "condescension" as a reference to Christ. By analogy with Assumption referring to the Mother of God, "condescension" refers to the Son of God. According to Christian doctrine God "condescended to descend" in the form of Christ, the Word made Flesh. In line 14 ED uses "condescension" in this way, implying her "heretical" doubt that Christ is a "condescension" of God. She says here that if Christian doctrine —the Holy Word—be true, then her own Word is illusory, a dead letter as it were. This is the logic used by Christian missionaries in Asia, who say that since their religion is true, then Buddhism is false; Buddha mind is no more than a heathen sin.

At this point we need to undertake a close reading of P-1651.

THEISM

A WORD MADE FLESH

> In the beginning was the Word, & the Word was with
> God, & the Word was God.
>
> And the Word was made flesh, & dwelt among us, ... full of
> grace & truth.
>
> John 1: 1, 14

ED's reference to the Gospel of John gives a focus to her own idea of who she herself is, & why she is writing her own gospel (or sutra). I frequently call ED a poet/witness, because her transcendentalist poetry bears witness to her own experience of life as higher consciousness. In John 1: 6-8 we read:

> There was a man sent from God whose name was
> John. The same came for a witness, to bear witness
> of the Light... He was not that Light, but was sent
> to bear witness of that Light.

These statements may be accurately adapted to mean ED herself:

> There was a woman sent from God, whose name was
> ED. The same came for a witness, to bear witness of
> the Light. She was not that Light, but was sent to
> bear witness of that Light.

ED's transcendentalist poetry is her way of putting non-ego experience into words. This is the Flesh made Word: she, the poet, has an experience in the flesh, & translates it into words. Ideally the reader's understanding will become the Word made Flesh, i.e., ED's Word will resonate with the reader who has shared that same experience, as she says in P-842:

> Good to know, & not tell,
> Best, to know & tell,
> Can one find the rare Ear
> Not too dull –

Ego-transcendence is more or less "illegal" in an egocentric society, & substances that promote it are quickly outlawed. This is why ED refers to "ecstasies of stealth" [line 6]. This is the stealth of P-1553:

> Bliss is the plaything of the child –
> The secret of the man
> The sacred stealth of Boy & Girl
> Rebuke it if we can

In P-129 she early recognizes the potential of ego-transcendence as a "Stealthy Cocoon":

> Cocoon above! Cocoon below!
> Stealthy Cocoon, why hide you so
> What all the world suspect?

In lines 5-8 ED recognizes that each transcendentalist ["Each one of us"] has tasted this "debated" food, this manna, dispensed to the "specific strength" of each one's ability to digest it.

The Gospel of St. John begins with the famous declaration, "In the beginning was the Word, & the Word was with God, & the

Word was God." "Word" is the translation of Gk. Logos, meaning 1) the rational principle that governs the universe, & 2) the second person of the Trinity. From the viewpoint of the transcendentalist, neither Christ nor the Buddha is unique in the ability to experience unconditioned awareness. The Buddha himself said, in effect, "If I can do this, everyone can do it." In the West, however, Christ became the personification of God, uniquely endowed, "that all men through him might believe" (John I: 7).

Thus I call ED an "accidental Buddhist," for she experienced ego-transcendence as an archetypal awareness available to us all, as did the Buddha. She herself was the witness embodying —i.e., in her own body, her own flesh—the logos of her poetry.

A crucial change she makes in the biblical text is the definite article: John says, "The Word made Flesh"; she says, "A Word made Flesh:, thereby de-Christianizing the biblical reference. "A Word made Flesh" is here her description of ego-transcendence, which, she, is "seldom / And tremblingly partook." The reference to her episodes of transcendence as "seldom" is repeated in P-1452, "infrequency":

> Your thoughts don't have words every day
> They come a single time
> Like signal esoteric sips
> Of the communion Wine
> Which while you taste so native seems
> So easy so to be
> You cannot comprehend its price
> Nor its infrequency

Nor does she only "report" her experience, as she reports in line 3 of the present poem. When she does report it, she knows that her Word "breathes distinctly" (line 9), as her readers readily recognize, for her poetic style is unmistakable. It is also coherent, or "cohesive" (line 11), like the logos driving it. Egocentric commentators would not agree, but that is not ED's fault.

576

I prayed, at first, a little Girl,
Because they told me to –
But stopped, when qualified to guess
How prayer would feel – to me –

If I believed God looked around,
Each time my Childish eye
Fixed full, & steady, on his own
In Childish honesty –

And told him what I'd like, today,
And parts of his far plan
That baffled me –
The mingled side
Of his Divinity –

And often since, in Danger,
I count the force 'twould be
To have a God so strong as that
To hold my life for me

Till I could take the Balance
That tips so frequent, now,
It takes me all the while to poise –
And then – it doesn't stay –

THEISM

A PSYCHOLOGICAL SELF-PORTRAIT

This poem makes a pair with P-476 ("I meant to have but modest needs"), for in both of them ED reminisces about her early religious faith. In the earlier poem she characterizes her prayers as expressing the conventional desire for the contentment that the Christian faith brings with it. One is content to be "saved," & to expect heaven as a reward. It would be enough, she says, to pray for salvation, & she would be graced with contentment:

> It would suffice my Prayer
> But just for One – to stipulate –
> And Grace would grant the Pair –

In the present poem ED recognizes that the habit of saying her prayers was part of the "socialization" imposed on all children:

> I prayed, at first, a little Girl,
> Because they told me to –

Being skeptical & empirical by temperament, she soon decided that she herself was the best judge of the value of praying:

> But stopped, when qualified to guess
> How prayer would feel – to me –

Given her active critical faculty, it did not take long for her to question the naïve belief in God as the Man Upstairs monitoring your every move:

> If I believed God looked around,
> Each time my Childish eye
> Fixed full, & steady, on his own
> In Childish honesty –

Elsewhere ED satirizes the idea of God as an individual, a Cosmic King keeping track. In P-413 he is a "Telescope" in the sky; in P-900 he is "that Bold Person"; in P-324 he is "a noted Clergyman."

In stanza three ED continues to characterize her youthful "dialogue" with God; she told him, she says, "what I'd like today." A great many American believers never outgrow this childish notion. Typical is Elizabeth Taylor: "I pray to God all the time… We have a conversational relationship, & those conversations calm my fears."*

ED expresses her "bafflement" at Jehovah's "far plan":

> And parts of his far plan
> That baffled me –
> The mingled side
> Of his Divinity –

To this day I myself am baffled by the explanation that God appeared on earth as his Son in order to redeem sinful humanity by having himself executed. ED's bafflement was precocious, & experienced not as the inability to grasp a truth, but rather as a suspicion of fallibility; the elders could be all wet.

---

* Ellis Amburn, <u>Elizabeth Taylor: The Most Beautiful Woman in the World</u>, 296.

In stanza four ED thinks about what it would be like to be a dependent, as the faithful consider themselves:

> And often since, in Danger,
> I count the force 'twould be
> To have a God so strong as that
> To hold my life for me

A "strong God" is a Father Protector who "holds your life for you." But since the ego-self is an illusion, its projections are in vain. There is no Bodyguard in the Sky.

In the final stanza ED uses the metaphor of Libra:

> Till I could take the Balance
> That tips so frequent, now,
> It takes me all the while to poise –
> And then – it doesn't stay –

As a Libran, I myself have a special affinity for this archetype. It refers to Psyche as a never-ending seesaw between ego-consciousness & the unconscious. ED, with her temperament for non-ego attitudes, would easily intuit this meaning for Libra. Here she recognizes that more & more frequently the balance tips towards the unconscious —the creative unconscious—& it is becoming ever more difficult to find the "poise," to play the role of Emily Dickinson. Eventually, of course, she will finally give up any desire to regain the "poise" of being Emily Dickinson, allowing herself to become ED once & for all.

1543

Obtaining but our own Extent
In whatsoever Realm –
'Twas Christ's own personal Expanse
That bore him from the Tomb –

THEISM

PERSONAL EXPANSE

In P-1487 ("The Savior must have been") ED expresses her realization that Christ, like all great spiritual leaders, was "different" from the rest of us, not because he was divine (as Christians believe), but because he had actualized an ego-transcendent identity.* She was able to see this only because she herself had discovered ego-transcendence, & now knew that it is the very basis of all higher spirituality. (Egocentric spirituality generates "cults.")

Ego-transcendence makes possible the Individuation Process (Jung's term) whereby one forms a connection with the creative unconscious, one's instinctual self, transcending the local contingencies of time & space. In the present poem ED returns to this theme:

> Obtaining but our own Extent
> In whatsoever Realm –

Each creative individual discovers his or her "own Extent / In whatsoever Realm," which is to say the extent of one's own transcendent awareness "obtained" by faithful attention & mindfulness, in whatever walk of life. (A classic answer to the question, "What is Zen?" is "Attention, attention, attention!")

ED was acutely aware of one's personal consciousness in terms of "extent," her preferred terms being "circumference,"

---

* See our discussion of P-1467, in <u>Solitary Prowess</u>, pp. 174-6.

& "circuit."* She uses several other synonyms —circle, precinct, boundary, zone, sphere, latitude, breadth, width, etc.

ED's use of "extent" in the present poem is part & parcel of an ongoing awareness of the scope of one's consciousness, of how it constantly expands & shrinks. As we say today, she was always into consciousness-raising.

Lines 3-4 of the present poem express ED's understanding that Jesus himself underwent ego-transcendence, or "personal Expanse":

'Twas Christ's own personal Expanse
That bore him from the Tomb –

The same is true of Mohammed & the Buddha. The personal Expanse of each resurrected him as the founder of a religion. On a more modest scale, the "personal Expanse" of our culture heroes —Lao Tzu, Gandhi, Beethoven, Sibelius—is what eternalizes them, bears them aloft from their Tombs. Dickinson's own personal Expanse, ED, is beginning to accomplish the same, & her many fans may one day awaken to ED.

---

* See our discussion in Solitary Prowess, pp. 174-6.

V. REALIZATION, ACTUALIZATION

Buddhists call ego-transcendence "realization." One who has experienced satori is a "realized" person, one who has fully recognized the dharma reality. This experience usually leads to thoughts about how to incorporate dharma values into everyday life, how to "actualize" them (as the Buddhists also say). After satori it is not easy to go back to business as usual. ED herself ponders this question in many poems, & in P-788 ("Joy to have merited the Pain") she even uses the term "actualize." She says that satire "notched itself upon her soul, leaving it "haunted." "Haunt" is her chosen word, as in her reference to Nature as "haunted house" (P-1400). For ED satori was the reunion of consciousness & Psyche, Mother Nature in human form. It never ceased to haunt her —that is, frequent her consciousness. Any numinous experience will "haunt" a person—that is what makes it numinous; ED recognizes this in P-788, saying that with satori, the Eternal Now, clock time dropped away, so as to "actualize" Haunting:

> To Haunt – till Time have dropped
> His last Decade away,
> And Haunting actualize – to last
> At least – Eternity –

Here, "actualize' means "to make current."*

This book has been about the shattering event of satori; but let us not leave Dickinson shattered. Let us end by recognizing how she actualized ED. This made her a stranger to those who saw only the woman they called Emily, & her discourse has suffered the same fate among commentators & biographers. ED, however, did not understand life to be a popularity contest, & her individuation proceeded without companionship, &, perhaps, even without poetry most of the time. These last two poems, P-646 & P-1615, concern the progressive raising of consciousness, with or without poetry.

---

* Cf. Spanish usage of <u>actualidades</u>, meaning "current events."

646

I think to Live – may be a Bliss
To those who dare to try –
Beyond my limit to conceive –
My lip – to testify –

I think the Heart I former wore
Could widen – till to me
The Other, like the little Bank
Appear – unto the Sea –

I think the Days – could every one
In Ordination stand –
And Majesty – be easier –
Than an inferior kind –

No numb alarm – lest Difference come –
No Goblin – on the Bloom –
No start in Apprehension's Ear,
No Bankruptcy – no Doom –

But Certainties of Sun –
Midsummer – in the Mind –
A steadfast South – upon the Soul –
Her Polar time – behind –

The Vision – pondered long –
So plausible becomes
That I esteem the fiction – real –
The Real – fictitious seems –

How bountiful the dream –
What Plenty – it would be –
Had all my Life but been Mistake
Just rectified – in Thee

Alfred Habegger, ED's recent biographer, regards this poem as containing a reference to a romantic crisis involving an unidentified man (line 5, "the Heart I former wore"), & says that Dickinson "had come to regard the crisis as her life's transforming event."*

It is extraordinary that a negative, egocentric crisis should be regarded as the transforming even of Dickinson's life, considering the fact that the transformation of Emily Dickinson into ED, the Higher Self, generated a lifetime of incomparable transcendent poetry, the bulk of which celebrates the human spirit with joy & exhilaration, or with an astute serenity. The "negative" poems, like those written by all realized transcendentalists, are those recognizing the Dark Night of the Soul.

ED's opening statement in this poem immediately contrasts ego & non-ego: life with or without Bliss:

> I think to Live – may be a Bliss
> To those who dare to try –
> Beyond my limit to conceive –
> My lip – to testify –

"Bliss" is one of ED's many names for satori (e.g., ecstasy, exhilaration, intoxication, enchantment, transport, glory, rapture, etc.). P-1553 offers an especially good example of this, because of the connection with children:

> Bliss is the plaything of the child –
> The secret of the man
> The sacred stealth of Boy & Girl
> Rebuke it if we can

---

* My Wars Are Laid Away in Books, 422.

Small children have not yet fully emerged from their immersion in the unconscious mind, & their close connection with Mother Nature in the form of Psyche.

P-1179 expresses the Dark Night of the Soul as the "divine loss" of "a Bliss":

> Of so divine a Loss
> We enter but the Fain,
> Indemnity for Loneliness
> That such a Bliss has been.

Satori not only enlightens the mind, it opens the heart. The Buddhists lay great stress on this, for compassion (karuna) flows from the open heart. In stanza two ED calls it "widening" the heart:

> I think the Heart I former wore
> Could widen – till to me
> The Other, like the little Bank
> Appear – unto the Sea –

This metaphor of the small stream & the ocean appears later, in P-1210:

> The Sea said "Come" to the Brook –
> The Brook said "Let me grow" –
> The Sea said "Then you will be a Sea –
> I want a Brook – Come now"!

"Oceanic consciousness" is a traditional term for ego-transcendence ("dalai lama" means "oceanic lama"), & is so well known that Freud, the egocentric thinker par excellence, saw fit to trivialize it — for which Alan Watts takes him to task:

Freud designated the longing for the return to the oceanic consciousness of the womb as the nirvana-principle, & his followers have persistently confused all ideas of transcending the ego with mere loss of "ego strength."*

ED herself, having experienced the wonders of satori, naturally regarded Emily Dickinson as Our Miss Brooks.

Beginning with stanza three, ED fantasizes the actualized life:

> I think the Days – could every one
> In Ordination stand –
> And Majesty – be easier –
> Than an inferior kind –

Every day would be "ordained," invested with spiritual authority, & would easily come to have a "Majesty."

Royalty is an archetype of ego-transcendence, & appears frequently in ED's discourse, as in P-290, where the night sky

> Infects my simple spirit
> With Taints of Majesty –

In stanza four of the present poem ED imagines the absence of what the Buddhists call duhkah, the suffering characteristic of ego:

> No numb alarm – lest Difference come –
> No goblin – on the Bloom –
> No start in Apprehension's Ear,
> No Bankruptcy – no Doom –

In the actualized life, duhkah would be succeeded by "Certainties of Sun,"

---

* Psychotherapy East & West, 31.

Midsummer – in the Mind –
A steadfast South – upon the Soul –
Her Polar time – behind –

Which is to say the Eternal Now.

In stanza six ED's version of actualization becomes more & more "plausible":

The Vision – pondered long –
So plausible becomes
That I esteem the fiction – real –
The real – fictitious seems –

She did indeed "ponder long" this vision, & eventually the reality of ED won out over the fiction of Emily Dickinson.

The final stanza addresses Buddha Mind:

How bountiful the Dream –
What Plenty – it would be –
Had all my Life but been Mistake
Just rectified – in Thee

She describes here the feeling of anyone who experiences realization, that a "mistake" has just been "rectified." The small child, being "socialized" in a given time & place, is an "unsuspecting Heir" (P-1090); that, however, is all a big mistake rectified by ego-transcendence.

373

I'm saying every day
"If I should be a Queen, tomorrow" –
I'd do this way –
And so I deck, a little,

If it be, I wake a Bourbon,
None on me, bend supercilious –
With "This was she –
Begged in the Market place –
Yesterday."

Court is a stately place –
I've heard men say –
So I loop my apron, against the Majesty
With bright Pins of Buttercup –
That not to plain –
Rank – overtake me –

And perch my tongue
On Twigs of singing – rather high –
But his, might be my brief Term
To qualify –

Put from my simple speech all plain word –
Take other accents, as such I heard
Though but for the Cricket – just,
And but for the Bee –
Not in all the Meadow –
One accost me –

Better to be ready –
Than did next morn
Meet me in Aragon –
My old Gown – on –

And the surprised Air
Rustics – wear –
Summoned – unexpectedly –
To Exeter -

SUMMONED UNEXPECTEDLY

In this unusually discursive poem Dickinson, having experienced realization (satori), fantasizes becoming actualized for good, as ED. Following her coronation (P-356, "The Day that I was crowned"), she imagines the possibility of becoming installed in the dharma, as Queen:

> I'm saying every day
> "If I should be a Queen, tomorrow" –

ED's readers are familiar with her several references to this royal, or queenly, identity. In P-285 ("The Robin's my Criterion for Tune"), ED, as poetry, accounts for her provincial discourse:

> Because I see – New Englandly –
> The Queen, discerns like me –
> Provincially –

In P-346 ("Not probable"), a cry of anguish out of the dark night of the soul apostrophizes ED:

> Oh, Groping feet –
> Oh Phantom Queen!

In P-458 ("Like Eyes that looked on Wastes") ED describes the conflict between Dickinson, "queen" of the ego-identity, & ED, Queen of the dharma-self:

> Neither – would be absolved –
> Neither would be a Queen
> Without the Other – Therefore –
> We perish – tho' We reign –

In the present poem Dickinson goes on to fantasize about her awakened potential as a divine right:

> If it be, I wake a Bourbon,
> None on me, bend supercilious –
> With "This was she –
> Begged in the Market place –
> Yesterday."

The Buddha himself said that ego-transcendence is inherently possible to us all. It is the human condition: "Everyone is a Buddha, whether aware of this of not." So this is indeed our divine right, our right by birth to become divine - or, as ED puts it in P-1692, "The right to perish," to experience ego-death.

Stanza three of the present poem contrasts the commoner & the noble:

> Court is a stately place –
> I've heard men say –
> So I loop my apron, against the Majesty
> With bright Pins of Buttercup –
> That not too plain –
> Rank – overtake me –

The "Rank" that might "overtake" her is what she calls "My second Rank" in P-508 ("I'm ceded") – chronologically the second identity (non-ego) after the first one, the ego-self she was "socialized" to accept out there in what everyone habitually calls the "real world."

In stanza four, following the reference to "Pins of Buttercup" (line 13), she specifies her vocation as "nature poet" as being a voice born out of a oneness with Mother Earth (mystical participation):

> And perch my Tongue
> On Twigs of signing – rather high –
> But this, might be my brief Term
> To qualify –

This evokes the classical haiku poets of Japan, where each haiku is a "brief Term / to qualify" as a dharma voice.

In stanza five ED considers the style of her discourse:

> Put from my simple speech all plain word –
> Take other accents, as such I heard
> Though but for the Cricket – just,
> And but for the Bee –
> Not in all the Meadow –
> One accost me –

I take "plain word" to mean conventional speech, as when we say "plain English," "calling a spade a spade." Plain ego-words when used for non-ego discourse, are no longer "plain speech," as ED commentators, the "puzzled scholars" (P-501), are forever reminding us. ED's speech is "simple," indeed, but far from "plain."*

She says that her oneness with "other accents" heard in Nature does not include the cricket & the bee, which I take to mean a deeper oneness with the Song of the Earth. The low, collective, nocturnal song of the crickets, & the mysterious tribal buzzing of the bees hidden within the hive – these are all unseen, &

---

* The poet Gustavo Adolfo Becquer (1836-70) is for me the Spanish counterpart of ED. He was a transcendentalist who also used a "simple speech," so much so that the critics called him "an angel with a concertina."

these tiny creatures do not "accost" us, like the skylark or the bobolink.

In the last two stanzas Dickinson admonishes herself to stay at the ready, because satori, like lightning, can strike again at any time, "summoning" us immediately to a completely outlandish venue (psychedelically as it were), such as a castle in Spain (Aragon), or to the venerable Norman cathedral at Exeter, housing the collection of ancient Anglo-Saxon poetry:

> Better to be ready –
> Than did next morn
> Meet me in Aragon –
> My old Gown – on –
>
> And the surprised Air
> Rustics – wear –
> Summoned – unexpectedly –
> To Exeter –

"Summoned – unexpectedly,' she says; no need to be caught unaware, clad in her "old Gown," as happens in P-712 ("Because I could not stop for Death". There, ego-death catches her unprepared:

> The Dews drew quivering & chill –
> For only Gossamer, my Gown –
> My Tippet – only Tulle –

"Summoned – unexpectedly" evokes ED's famous epitaph, supplied by herself: "Called Back." Physical death characteristically "summons" us unexpectedly – but so does ego-death. Be prepared! Don't try to pretend that satori is nothing more than a crazy dream.

633

When Bells stop ringing – Church – begins –
The Positive – of Bells –
When Cogs – stop – that's Circumference –
The Ultimate – of Wheels.

1008

How still the Bells in Steeples stand
Till swollen with the Sky
They leap upon their silver Feet
In frantic Melody!

THE TINTINNABULATION OF THE BELLS

P-633 is a terse example of how ED's outer circumstances make a unique connection with her inner life. Both of the poems cited here use church bells as a special metaphor for satori – which is to say that for the realized person the ringing bells evoke the sudden joyful experience of satori as an existential holiday / holy day of light, as in P-604:

> It may be Wilderness – without –
> Far feet of failing Men –
> But Holiday – excludes the night –
> And it is Bells – within –

In P-633, "When Bells stop ringing – Church – begins," ED makes an inspired connection between bell-ringing & church service. The one announces the other, just as realization announces, or maybe promises the possibility of actualization;

> When Bells stop ringing – Church – begins –
> The Positive – of Bells –

In P-1593 ED specifically connects bell-ringing with satori:

> The Bell within the steeple wild
> The flying tidings told –
> How much can come
> And much can go,
> And yet abide the World!

With ego-transcendence the everyday, conventional world of samsara vanishes as a viable reality ("How much can go"), & the non-ego reality of nirvana ("ego-extinction") floods consciousness ("How much can come"). There are the two alternate realities — & the world ever abides.

When you "come down" from satori, the "Bells stop ringing." With the end of satori, "Church begins." This is "The Positive — of Bells." The everyday life of actualizing Big Self is "church" for the realized person. It is what the Buddha called the Noble Eightfold Path — right thinking, right speaking, etc. By "right" is meant "non-ego."

In P-633 ED offers a second metaphor:

> When Cogs – stop – that's Circumference –
> The Ultimate – of wheels.

This is a clear metaphor, so long as one has a clear idea of what a cog is, & what it does. The Oxford Dictionary defines it as follows:

> 1. each of a series of projections on the edge of a wheel... transferring motion by engaging with another series. 2. An unimportant member of an organization.

ED uses "circumference" in the sense of "field of consciousness."* When a cogwheel is revolving, a full turn describes the circumference that transfers the motion, i.e., the direction of awareness. The little self is but a cog in the movement of psychic energy: when it describes a full turn, when it transfers the motion, that is "The Ultimate — of Wheels." At this point, church begins.

---

* See Solitary Prowess, 174-181.

1615

Oh what a Grace is this,
What Majesties of Peace,
That having breathed
The fine – ensuing Right
Without Diminuet Proceed!

FROM REALIZATION TO ACTUALIZATION: OUR ENSUING RIGHT

This late poem (c. 1884), terse as it is, addresses directly the issue of Actualization; indeed, its very terseness, like that of classical haiku, lends authority to the spiritual serenity free of rhetoric & discursiveness.

Buddhist adepts have always recognized Realization & Actualization as the two modes of dharma awareness. Uchiyana Roshi finds an analogy in love & marriage:

> To fall in love is ecstasy, but marriage is everyday life. Everyday life has rainy days, windy days, & stormy days. So you can't always be happy. It's the same with zazen. There are two kinds of zazen transmitted in Japan. One understands zazen as ecstasy & the other understands zazen as everyday life.*

Roshi B. Glassman, an elder of the American Buddhist community, calls Actualization "Continuous Practice":

> Say you have a realization of the oneness of life. If you stop right there, thinking there's nothing more to grasp, your conditioned ways of doing things will soon take over once again. But if you continue to practice after the initial enlightenment experience, it

---

* <u>Buddhadharma</u> (Spring, 2003), 12.

      will continue to unfold & broaden... That's what we
      call Continuous Practice.*

ED's most dramatic dharma poems are naturally those born of satori, the bolt from the blue; the poetry of actualization, subtle & quietly satisfying, must be discovered little by little, leading one to feel that this is ED at her maturest.

ED's readers are familiar with her poems in definition (e.g., the famous P-254, "'Hope' is the thing with feathers"—& these are frequently epigrammatic (e.g., P-1268, re: Eloquence, "when the Heart / Has not a Voice to spare"). Her ability to forge trenchant definitions is certainly related to her love of her lexicon (Webster's Dictionary): in this way she was a Lexicographer of a Higher Order (To adapt a favorite phrase of Thoreau's). Nowhere is this more patent than in the present brief poem, where she recognizes the utter peace that comes with awakening to the dharma as a continuous experience:

> Oh what a Grace is this,
> What Majesties of Peace,

ED, like all dharma <u>people</u>, was ever aware of the identity of breath & spiritus, as when she say, in P-1733, one of her last poems, "breathing is the only work / To be enacted now." In the present poem she makes the same point:

> That having breathed
> The fine – ensuing Right

Enlightenment consists of experiencing the identity of breath & Spirit, whereupon you realize that this is the inherent <u>right</u> of every human being. As the Buddha said, everyone is a Buddha,

---

*   Tricycle (Fall, 1999), 73.

even those who do not "realize" it. It is the inborn right of every living creature to follow its instinctual nature — & the instinctual nature of the human being is to individuate beyond the limitations imposed by the social identity.

After realization comes actualization, which is the "follow-through": ED nails this. It is our "ensuing Right." Using the musical term Diminuet (diminudendo) she rejoices in the way the dharma symphony "proceeds" apace:

> Without Diminuet Proceed!

Actualizing non-ego nurtures the Song of the Earth, without regard for the passing of the time.

BIBLIOGRAPHY

Allen, Rupert C. Emily Dickinson, Accidental Buddhist. Victoria, BC: Trafford, 2007.

------------. Solitary Prowess: The Transcendentalist Poetry of Emily Dickinson. San Francisco: Saru Press, 2005.

Amburn, Ellis. Elizabeth Taylor: The Most Beautiful Woman in the World. New York: Cliff St. Books, 2000.

Baynes, H. G. Mythology of the Soul. New York: Humanities Press, 1955.

Buddhadharma. Boulder, Colorado.

Dickinson, Emily. The Complete Poems of Emily Dickinson. Thomas H. Johnson, ed. Boston: Little, Brown, & Co., 1960.

------------. Selected Letters. Thomas H. Johnson, ed. Cambridge: The Belknap Press, 1958.

Doyle, Arthur Conan. The Complete Sherlock Holmes. New York: Doubleday, 1906.

Graves, Robert. Difficult Questions, Easy Answers. London: Cassell, 1972.

Habegger, Alfred. My Wars Are Laid Away in Books. New York: Modern Library, 2002.

Keown, Damien. A Dictionary of Buddhism. New York: Oxford Univ. Press, 2003.

McCleary, John. The Hippie Dictionary. Berkeley: Ten Speed Press, 2002.

Narayan, R. K. The Financial Expert. London: Vintage, 2001.

Shambhala Sun. Boulder, Colorado.

Thoreau, Henry David. Journal. Vols. 7-20 in The Writings of Henry David Thoreau. New York: Houghton Mifflin, 1906.

Tricycle: The Buddhist Review. New York.

USA Weekend. New York.

Utne. Topeka.

Watts, Alan. Psychotherapy East & West. New York: Ballantine Books, 1961.

Wolff, Cynthia. Emily Dickinson. New York: Knopf, 1986.

Words for the Hour: A New Anthology of American Civil War Poetry. Faith Barrett & Cristanne Miller, eds. Amherst: Univ. of Massachusetts Press, 2005.

Zimmer, Heinrich. The Art of Indian Asia. New York: Bollingen, 1955.

GENERAL INDEX

Alpert, Richard, 56

INDEX OF FIRST LINES

(Asterisk indicates full quotation)

347